1981

Edith Wharton's
Argument with America

Edith Wharton's
Argument with America

Elizabeth Ammons

The University of Georgia Press
Athens

Set in 10 on 13 point Tiffany Light type
Printed in the United States of America

Library of Congress Cataloging in Publication Data

Ammons, Elizabeth.
  Edith Wharton's argument with America.
  Includes index.
  1. Wharton, Edith Newbold Jones, 1862–1937—
Criticism and interpretation.   I. Title.
PS3545.H16Z54   813'.52   79-48000
            ISBN 0-8203-0513-8

The publication of this work was made possible in part
through a grant from the National Endowment for the
Humanities, a federal agency whose mission is to
award grants to support education, scholarship, media
programming, libraries, and museums in order to bring
the results of cultural activities to the general public.

For Samuel John Miller
and Mary Louise Schroeder Miller

Contents

Preface

E dith Wharton came of age as a novelist at a point in American literary and social history when invigorated debate on "the woman question" quickened the national literature. She not only entered that debate; she was one of its key figures. Her fiction records her public argument with America on the issue of freedom for women over more than three decades of some of the most significant upheaval and change and finally stasis in the history of women in the United States. Wharton's argument is not simple. It begins in the 1890s uncertainly, develops during the years of the progressive movement into a highly sophisticated critique that fuses sociological, economic, psychological, and anthropological perspectives, reverses much of itself and grows conservative in the 1920s, and comes to rest in the early 1930s, mystically. It is both a record of one brilliant and intellectually independent woman's thinking about women and a map of feminism's ferment and failure in America in the decades surrounding the Great War.

My discussion of that argument is organized chronologically. The first five chapters are devoted to the evolution of Wharton's point of view during the Progressive Era, which saw her produce her best work, the novels through *The Age of Innocence*; the last two chapters are devoted to analysis of the surprising shift in her argument about women in the Roaring Twenties.

The opening chapter, "Fin de Siècle," examines Wharton's

work before *The House of Mirth* (1905): her search for themes and her experiments with subject matter, her temptation to misandry (which she never fully conquered), her desire for commercial success, and her first attempts at political fiction about women. Chapter 2, "The New Woman," shows those political impulses maturing in her first full-length novels about America, *The House of Mirth* (1905) and *The Fruit of the Tree* (1907), two economic novels about the obstacles to freedom facing young women in the United States—popular enthusiasm about the New Woman notwithstanding. The following chapter, "Love," discusses how after a significant lapse in her productivity she moved her argument beyond economics in her next long fictions, exploring in the unlikely companion pieces *Ethan Frome* (1911) and *The Reef* (1912) what she now understood as the psychological bondage of romantic love and thus deepening her argument by bringing in psychosexual considerations. Chapter 4, "The Business of Marriage," shows Wharton's argument reaching its maturity in *The Custom of the Country* (1913): the satiric novel is her tour de force on the marriage question, portraying marriage in ruthless mercantile terms and making of romantic love a joke. Chapter 5, "The War," examines the completion of this major phase of Wharton's career in *Summer* (1917) and *The Age of Innocence* (1920), both written in reaction to the horror of the First World War, and showing that influence in their anthropological rhetorics, but nevertheless remaining Progressive Era books in their ardent commitment to the principle of freedom for women.

My last two chapters discuss the war's profound but delayed effect on Edith Wharton. I discuss how it stimulated the marked conservative shift in her argument and concomitant decline in quality of her novels about the 1920s (which has been amply remarked in the existing criticism but not really accounted for). Chapter 6, "Mothers and Flappers," analyzes her reactionary endorsement of motherhood as woman's best and highest mission in life during the decade that followed the First World War and explains—historically and politically as well as biographically—this dramatic and furious change in Edith Wharton's argument with America. The last chapter, "The Mothers," is short and reflective. It examines Wharton's final and intricately worked-out image of the Mothers, symbol of female primacy and spiritual matriarchy borrowed from Goethe's *Faust*, and takes seriously these last thoughts and feelings on woman's ancient, maternal potency—thoughts that in 1932 show her, like Faulkner in America or Helen Diner in Germany, addressing a new set of issues, tantalizing in their implications but finally left by the aging Wharton for others to mine.

I am grateful to the Mellon Foundation for a fellowship that gave me part of the time I needed for work on this book. Also my thanks are due the National Endowment for the Humanities, whose funding of the Edith Wharton Project, for which I served as a consultant, directly aided my work. For permission to use manuscript material in the Edith Wharton Collection at Yale University I am grateful to the Beinecke Rare Book and Manuscript Library; for permission to draw on my own published essays on Wharton I wish to thank the editors of *American Literature, Studies in American Fiction*, and *Criticism*. Friends and colleagues have been generous with suggestions and criticism as I worked on the manuscript and although, of course, I alone claim its faults, I wish to thank especially Nina Baym and Dorothy Berkson, and also David Cavitch and Suzanne Graver. Most of all I am grateful to my husband, Mark. It is my good fortune to have had the support and encouragement of these people.

E. A.

Fin de Siècle

At the Chicago World's Fair in 1893 there was an entire building devoted to women. It was conceived by women, managed by women, designed by a woman architect, and decorated by women artists and painters, among them the young Mary Cassatt. Called the Woman's Building, it contained nothing but work by women, and its purpose, in the words of one of its enthusiastic contemporary historians, was "to dispell the prejudices and misconceptions, to remove the vexatious restrictions and limitations, which for centuries have held enthralled the sex."[1] The structure itself implied that the task would not be difficult: inside were hundreds of tributes and displays that testified to woman's potential by illustrating her past achievements in art, science, education, and manufacture. The project was a monument to women's heritage and a symbol that things were changing rapidly now that the twentieth century was almost at hand. As Mrs. Potter Palmer, president of the Women's Committee for the Exposition, declared in her speech at the fair's opening ceremonies in October 1892: "Even more important than the discovery of Columbus, which we are gathered together to celebrate, is the fact that the general government has just discovered woman."[2]

Edith Wharton never saw the Woman's Building. In 1893 she was decorating her new house at Land's End in Newport, Rhode Island, writing, entertaining occasional houseguests, and fighting off the spells of depression that would, a year later, result in a nervous collapse so severe that she would be incapacitated for close to two years. Her distance in 1893 from even so conservative a phenomenon as the Woman's Building was immense; at the age of thirty-one she was just becoming aware of her own situation as a woman. Moreover, she was not by disposition or upbringing a person to join with any group of people working toward a social goal, much less get out and campaign or march. Until the First World War taught her how to work corporately, she remained the perfect product of her old New York rearing which told her to refrain from personal, direct political actions and statements.

Many Americans, in contrast, were vocal. After thirty years of steady but comparatively static activity, the Woman Movement, as it was called at the time, picked up widespread support in the United States between the early nineties and the end of the Great War. The mood showed itself politically in suffrage campaigns directed toward passage of the Nineteenth Amendment, which finally succeeded in 1920. Socially it was manifest more variously in changes ranging from the gradual abandonment of the corset or the slow relaxation of the taboo against a respectable woman's earning her own living, to the organized efforts of newly founded women's clubs working on behalf of numerous reforms—pure food and drug acts, conservation of the nation's forests, protective legislation for child laborers, the installation of female matrons in women's prisons, the creation of free kindergartens. Wharton was not among the activists. Separated by class and temperament, she held herself aloof on the question of the vote; and she certainly joined no women's club.

Yet she was affected profoundly by the Woman Movement, and with *The House of Mirth*, a best-seller in 1905, she became one of its most unlikely yet important independent thinkers and critics. The culture at large boasted symbols of progress like the world-famous Woman's Building or the amazonian Gibson Girl, announcements each of the modern woman's freedom from Victorian strictures. After all, the New

Woman could work outside the home in dignified occupations, she could marry whom she pleased, she could divorce if she had to, she could even swim and smoke cigarettes if she were truly daring. With this enthusiasm in the air, Edith Wharton sounded a sour, dissenting note. Relentlessly she examined the disjunction between popular optimism and the reality as she saw it. Typical women in her view—no matter how privileged, nonconformist, or assertive (indeed, often in proportion to the degree in which they embodied those qualities)—were not free to control their own lives, and that conviction became the foundation of her argument with American optimism for more than twenty years. She agreed that the position of women in American society was the crucial issue of the new century; she did not believe that change was occurring. In her opinion the American woman was far from being a new or whole human being.

She did not arrive at her opinion quickly; it took her more than a decade to harness and understand fully her argument. Not until *The House of Mirth* in 1905 was she completely and coolly able to express the tragedy of woman's situation as she had come to see it: the waste, the crippling, the curtailment. Before that, for fifteen years she wandered, and on occasion groped, testing themes and situations in nearly three dozen short stories, the novella *Bunner Sisters* (not published until 1916), two very short novels *The Touchstone* (1900) and *Sanctuary* (1903), and one long historical romance, *The Valley of Decision* (1902). Much of this fiction, which is novice, and therefore perhaps all the more worth pausing over before turning to Wharton's mature work, records the author's personal misery. In the 1890s she was as yet so confused about her own life, and so unhappy, that the fiction itself is often confused, and often angry. The women she imagined are enmeshed in lives they detest; the issues involved are extravagant: entombment, deceit, entrapment, defamation, murder, betrayal. And the villain, almost always, is a man. Disciplining this anger had to be Edith Wharton's first task if she was to succeed as a writer.

The task would be far from simple. During the nineties and then in the first years of this century Wharton had basic things to discover about herself and to learn as a writer. Above all she had to find the public terms of her argument with America on the subject of woman. The expression of her individual pain finally could be only a beginning; she would, as she herself came to see, have to find ways to translate and transform her private fears and resentments into publicly arguable issues. And to do that, she would have to expand her vision and art, as she obviously set about doing. She wrote about women from widely different economic and social stations. She tried her hand at various popular forms of long fiction—flirting with muckraking in *Bunner Sisters*, trying out melodrama in *The Touchstone* and *Sanctuary*, attempting historical romance in *The Valley of Decision*. Conceptually—and this proved most important in the development of her career—she moved steadily closer to overtly political fiction, narratives that deal directly with the nature and distribution of power along sexual as well as social and economic lines. She began with a little parable in the mid-nineties, "The Valley of Childish Things," and arrived by 1905 at a full-length novel, *The House of Mirth*.

It is important to remember that Wharton was not alone in her work. The nineties saw a generation of women writers develop in America, and for many the decade was a time of exploration. Like their male counterparts—Hamlin Garland, Stephen Crane, Frank Norris—women publishing in the 1890s consciously experimented; they played with form, often preferring short sketches to long fictions, and frequently chose to work regionally. Rather than attempt huge panoramas they looked closely at isolated subcultures. Kate Chopin wrote of Creole mores in the deep South; Ellen Glasgow of life in Richmond and in New York City. Mary Austin and Gertrude Atherton, while not limiting themselves to regional material, wrote expertly of Westerners. Well-established Sarah Orne Jewett and Mary Wilkins Freeman studied rural New England. It was a decade friendly to serious women writers.

It was also a decade that was in the broadest sense highly political. Setting women writers apart historically, as Larzer Ziff has pointed out, was the fact that "to be a serious female author in the nineties was to be a writer of stories about women and their demands." Ziff remarks that for a woman writer "the condition of women inescapably had to be the material of her art."[3] The pages of *Scribner's* and the *Century*, the magazines that gave Edith Wharton her start, were thick with stories by women about women, and the best-seller charts showed the same pattern. As the Woman's Building exhibited early in the decade, there was new pride in women and great optimism about the future: not surprisingly, a new generation of readers tired of the tear-jerkers of their grandmothers' youth surfaced. Instead of *The Lamplighter* and *Tempest and Sunshine*, best-sellers that taught young ladies in the 1850s how to repress rebellion, readers in the nineties made best-sellers out of books such as *A Bachelor Maid* (1894) and *Patience Sparhawk and Her Times* (1895), adventure stories that show modern heroines rebelling against the past, successfully. Brave new women were invading fiction in the 1890s, and authors, by and large, had happy tales to tell.

But not Edith Wharton. In sharp contrast, most of her work in the 1890s focuses in one way or another on the pain of being a woman. Her governing themes rise from the recurrent situation of a heroine perceiving an enormous and cruel lack of fit between her personal expectations of life and the social reality. Where there is rebellion it almost always meets with failure. Wharton's first published story, "Mrs. Manstey's View" (*Scribner's Magazine*, 1891), is about powerlessness (an old woman is deprived of her one pitiful pleasure in life, her view) and failed rebellion; and although the heroine does have a moment of retaliation when she sets a construction site on fire, we are left with no Sarah Orne Jewett sentiment about old women's spunk. Even in this first fiction the new author was working toward an individual vision, unsentimental and unpleasant: her old woman dies under the illusion that she can control the circumstances of her life when, in fact, all she can do is stop men's shovels for one day.

It is very common even in Wharton's earliest stories for a woman abruptly to come face to face with some bitter disillusionment, which often turns on discovering that the man she loves, or thought she loved, is a fraud. The hero of a woman's dreams turns out to be a coward in "The Lamp of Psyche" and "The Twilight of a God." The passionate sharer of her revolutionary notions about free love turns out to be convention bound in "Souls Belated." The intellectual heroine of "The Muse's Tragedy" discovers that men cannot love her body and her mind; it must be one or the other. Perhaps the bleakest is "A Journey." The heroine is a frontier schoolteacher who gets married to broaden and deepen her lonely life, but the first thing her husband does is fall mortally ill; when we meet this bride in the story she is riding the night-train East to New York hoping that her new mate, now almost dead, will live through till morning. If not, she and the body will be put off at the nearest station. The man dies in his sleep and "A Journey," one of Wharton's most hopeless tales, maps the young woman's terror through the night as she manages to conceal the corpse. The dead marriage arrives safely in New York.

A number of Wharton's early stories, like "A Journey," show the depressing directions in which she was working as her first long fiction was taking shape. As her career went on she would take many of the same ideas and transform them into sophisticated political statements; but at the outset it was often despair, not argument, that was in control. Her imagination was engaged by the isolation and powerlessness of women, the failure of men to live up to women's expectations, the confinement of marriage for wives (yet the impossibility of "free" love in any highly organized society), the suspect ideal of feminine self-sacrifice, the loneliness of the "intellectual" woman. Taken as a whole the decade was a trying period for Wharton. She was wretched in her marriage; she was unsteady in her art. Although all of her work had promise, much of it was uneven: on the subject of woman, clearly the subject of keenest interest to her, she was not yet able to lower her voice.

By the end of the decade, she herself realized that she had been screaming. She wrote to her editor, Edward Burlingame, at Scribner's in 1898 concerning the pieces for her first collection of short stories, *The Greater Inclination*:

As to the old stories of which you speak so kindly, I regard them as the excesses of youth. They were all written at the top of my voice, and "The Fullness of Life" is one long shriek. I may not write any better, but at least I hope that I write in a lower key, and I fear that the voice of those early tales will drown all the others; it is for that reason that I prefer not to publish them.[4]

Although "The Fullness of Life" had made its author ecstatic early in the nineties when she learned that it was going to appear in print, thus bringing to two her published works in 1893, it was dropped out of the 1898 anthology. No doubt Wharton resisted anthologizing the story because it was immature. But also, as her biographer R. W. B. Lewis suggests, "The Fullness of Life" too nakedly reveals its author's private disillusionment with her own marriage.

Edith Newbold Jones married Edward ("Teddy") Wharton in 1885 apparently without much thought beyond the fact— as would be normal enough for a young woman of her background—that he was handsome, good-natured, and shared her love for travel. The story she went on to write about this marriage eight years later, and then suppress,

"The Fullness of Life," is about a dead woman who must decide whether to spend eternity with the kind but loutish man she has married. She chooses in the end against personal happiness, determining to wait for her husband, whose need and affection she feels she cannot betray. The story is transparent psychologically. It speaks of the author's wish in the early nineties that she herself were dead, and of her simultaneous fear that maybe she *was* dead—or might as well be. Yet it also speaks of her compassion for her husband and of her guilt. The story protests that she would not, could not, leave Teddy. In actuality she could and did, formalizing their long estrangement in an upsetting divorce in 1913. "The Fullness of Life," twenty years before the divorce, dreads and tries to deny that inevitability at the same time that it tries to assuage the guilt of even fantasizing about leaving one's husband. Wharton, whose own unhappiness led to a series of nervous breakdowns in the 1890s, has her heroine make up for her psychological desertion in this life by promising to stay close to her husband in the next.

Of the stories Wharton wrote in the nineties many, along with "The Fullness of Life," can be read as veiled fiction about the author. Images of entrapment and isolation and of vague persecution certainly reflect what Edith Wharton must have been feeling about her own life in the years that saw the nineteenth century come to a close. But what is important about the best of her work in these years is the way she was learning to channel those feelings to create a public argument out of her private fear and anger. After "The Fullness of Life," for Wharton professionally the decade might be thought of as calisthenics, and although many of her short stories and all of her attempts at long fiction fell short of what she would write from *The House of Mirth* on, a few of her stories about women, like "A Journey," were beautifully conceived and perfectly executed, providing glimpses of what later years would bring. She was struggling against the temptation toward blunt misandry, an impulse that plagued her work from the beginning and one that she was never able to eradicate entirely; and much of what she wrote in the nineties lacked political clarity and subtlety. Yet on several occasions she produced social criticism of unmistakable vision, fiction that reflected the difficult transition she was making from her personal "shriek" in "The Fullness of Life" in 1893 to her sophisticated public argument on the woman question in *The House of Mirth* in 1905.

Among such work, even standing at the front probably, is her unusual parable, "The Valley of Childish Things." The parable is a cynical and sure-handedly political piece that appeared in the *Century* magazine in the summer of 1896, just three years after the Woman's Building in Chicago had officially bragged about woman's bright new future.

A year after the World's Fair in Chicago, Scribner's came out with a lavish new two-volume almanac for women, which is worth describing here because it could very well have served as Wharton's barometer of popular opinion for her parable. She almost certainly knew *The Woman's Book* (1894). Not only was Scribner's her publisher, but one of the chapters in the second volume was written by her sister-in-law and dear friend, Mary ("Minnie") Cadwalader Jones, who is also quoted at length in the opening chapter of the first volume.[5] Wharton's own *House of Mirth* and *The Fruit of the Tree*, as I will discuss later, show an indebtedness to the ideas of her sister-in-law as they appear in this almanac. But even in the unlikely event that Wharton never saw a copy of the book (and, for instance, simply shared Minnie Jones's interests by accident or as the result of conversations), the spirit of *The Woman's Book*—its optimism—is exactly what she attacks in her parable about the New Woman in 1896.

The almanac, like the Woman's Building it is quick to admire,[6] is unmistakably up-to-date. On the conservative side it gives the usual tips on etiquette, housekeeping, fashion, and so forth. But *The Woman's Book* does not place those subjects first. The opening chapter, instead, discusses "Occupations for Women":

The New Fields of Work Open.—Art Study and Art Workers.—Women Architects.—Teaching.—Typewriting and Stenography.—Women's Exchanges.—Occupations for the Inexperienced.—The Trained Nurse.—Women Physicians and Lawyers.—Newspaper Work and Pay.—Dressmaking and Millinery.—Work Done at Home.—The Stage as a Profession.—Novel Occupations Followed.—Women as Local Photographers.—How Women Workers are Swindled.[7]

The second chapter is about "Women and Their Business Affairs" (included is a section on "The Rights of Married Women"), and only then does discussion turn to "The Principles of Housekeeping" and other traditional topics. To be sure, because each chapter was written by a different person, the two volumes are full of contradictions. Dress-reform is called for in one place and attacked in another; equal pay for equal work is recommended by one author and considered ridiculous by another. But on one thing there is consensus: great changes have taken place in the lives of American women. *The Woman's Book* scoffs at what it calls "the old-time fiction to the effect that woman was a tender flower, blooming only when sheltered from the world, and likely either to droop or lose its fragrance when brought into contact with a vulgar, work-a-day, money-grubbing world."[8] The American woman in 1894, according to Scribner's new almanac, stood at the beginning of a new era.

Wharton's cynical parable about the New Woman is short and begins quaintly: "Once upon a time a number of children lived together in the Valley of Childish Things, playing all manner of delightful games, and studying the same lesson books. But one day," Wharton tells us, "a little girl, one of their number, decided that it was time to see something of the world about which the lesson books had taught her; and as none of the children cared to leave their games, she set out alone to climb the pass which led out of the valley." The girl manages the difficult trip into the outer world where "she saw cities and men, and learned many useful arts, and in so doing grew to be a woman." She decides to return to the valley with her new knowledge and skills; on the arduous way back she meets a man, one of her old playmates—a "dull" boy when they were young but now a visionary like herself, with plans for the valley of "building bridges and draining swamps and cutting roads through the jungle." The newly grown-up woman had similar plans and resolves to work together with the man after they complete their exhausting journey. She does not get the chance. The children in the valley, although glad at first to see her, soon resent her maturity; at her approach they move off with their toys. She locates her fellow traveler, "who was the only grown man in the valley,"

but he was on his knees before a dear little girl with blue eyes and a coral necklace, for whom he was making a garden out of cockle-shells and bits of glass and broken flowers stuck in the sand.

The little girl was clapping her hands and crowing (she was too young to speak articulately); and when she who had grown to be a woman laid a hand on the man's shoulder, and asked him if he did not want to set to work with her building bridges, draining swamps, and cutting roads through the jungle, he replied that at that particular moment he was too busy.

As she turned away, he added in the kindest possible way, "Really, my dear, you ought to have taken better care of your complexion."[9]

Wharton's bitter parable first summarizes the position she would hold for many years: her commitment to a healthy, productive New Woman yet her conviction that America, rhetoric and world's fairs aside, continued to prefer infantile females. She would express the idea in 1907 in *The Fruit of the Tree*, in 1920 in *The Age of Innocence*, in 1928 in *The*

Children. It is one paradigm of her lifelong argument with American culture on the subject of woman. She would never change her mind on this point.

Throughout her long career Edith Wharton was able to imagine very few happy endings. Other authors showed women escaping in droves from bad matches into happy ones (the acceptable way to do this was to have the tyrannical first husband die) and thus they affirmed at one and the same time woman's right to be happy and self-determined and society's insistence that the highest estate for her was the married one. But as Wharton was coming to see it in the nineties, though of course she was not alone in her view, men's expectations of wives and modern women's expectations of themselves could be vastly different matters. Men, like the faceless clod in "The Valley of Childish Things," were afraid of strong women; they did not want mates who were their equals. They wanted wives less intelligent and less sophisticated than themselves. In part Wharton may have been generalizing from her own impressions about reactions to her. She was a brilliant woman who, as *The Touchstone* in 1900 would hint, could probably see herself scaring the men she met (of course she scared many women too). But whatever her route to the idea, and given her own marriage it could not have been entirely biographical, the belief that men purposefully sought out mates weaker than themselves stayed with her all her life, taking on new contours and different significances as her career developed, but nevertheless remaining a key concept from *Bunner Sisters* in the 1890s to *The Gods Arrive* in the 1930s.

For *Bunner Sisters*, her first attempt at long fiction, victimization of women by a depraved man was the subject Wharton chose; and in 1892, with just one published fiction behind her, she sent the piece to *Scribner's* magazine. The novella was not accepted for publication, on the grounds that it was too depressing. Not that Burlingame said as much; rather he hedged, diplomatically, by saying that fine as the novella was it lacked a cheerful juncture at which to split the tale into two installments. Wharton on her side long remained fond of the story, including it in her 1916 collection *Xingu and Other Stories*. Still *Bunner Sisters* is most fairly thought of as beginner's work and Burlingame was correct about one thing. The novella is depressing.

The story Wharton tells is as sordid as the one Stephen Crane would be able to publish one year later, *Maggie: A Girl of the Streets* (1893),only by paying out of his own pocket and using a pseudonym (and even then *Maggie* sold very badly). Clearly, American readers wanted exploitation to end in pretty visions of reform. But Wharton, like Crane, was not drawn to palliatives—and the price she paid was to have the publication of *Bunner Sisters* postponed twenty-four years. Both authors may have been highly melodramatic and in many ways naive in what they had to say in the nineties about life in the slums; but at the same time each must be given credit for avoiding the kind of mush about honest poor women that Alice Hegan Rice could so easily publish in *Mrs. Wiggs of the Cabbage Patch* at the end of the decade.

Set in the 1870s, Wharton's grim story is about two pathetic women, Ann Eliza and Evelina Bunner, who are middle-aged spinsters living in the back of a small sundries shop in the basement of a New York tenement. Their existence is crimped and drab, but at least they have some small savings and each other. Then Mr. Ramy comes along. He courts the timid sisters and, in a parody of Howells's subplot in *The Rise of Silas Lapham*, proposes to the wrong one, who immediately sacrifices her own happiness to her sister's and refuses the offer. Stolid Mr. Ramy does not mind. One Bunner sister is as good as the next for his purposes. He marries Evelina to get at the sisters' money (which amounts to much less than he thought) and separates them by moving with his bride to St. Louis. There he reveals his addiction to opium, runs off with a younger woman, and leaves Evelina (whose name is no doubt intended to remind us of the first woman whose gullibility was exploited) pregnant and destitute. She returns to New York to die and leave Ann Eliza, now a pauper, walking the streets in search of a saleswoman opening in a market that wants nothing but healthy, attractive, young clerks.

Conceptually, *Bunner Sisters* is a confused and camouflaged piece. Supposedly its purpose is to question self-sacrifice as an ideal. Ann Eliza, in the penultimate chapter, confronts "for the first time in her life . . . the awful problem of the inutility of self-sacrifice. . . . Self-effacement for the good of others had always seemed to her both natural and necessary. . . . Now she perceived that to refuse the gifts of life does not ensure their transmission to those for whom they have been surrendered."[10] The problem with this sentiment is not only that it is too easy for Wharton, even in 1892. It is also specious. There have been no "gifts of life" to surrender, much less transmit, in *Bunner Sisters*. Ann Eliza's act and her moral awakening are irrelevant to Wharton's theme, which does not really have to do with the morality of self-sacrifice. It has to do with the character of Ramy. He is the "gift" and it is that gift, not the desire to give, that Edith Wharton attacks, although she does not admit it. To do so would be to admit how crudely misandrous this story is.

Wharton always had difficulty granting anything approaching full humanity to her male characters, and only a few achieve empathic complexity. Yet even for Wharton, Ramy is a monster. He is raw predator, a man who is utterly selfish, devious, sadistic, and remorseless; and although we see little of him, the drama is his, and he functions not as an individual but as a stock villain. The moral of *Bunner Sisters* is that woman is better off without man, no matter how pitifully meager her life.

In a world composed of two genders, categorical hatred of

either sex closes discussion; and in many of her short stories, and especially in the long fiction before 1905, Edith Wharton had to struggle with that fact. She had to move beyond the misandry that repeatedly distorted her work. Because patriarchal attitudes oppress women it does not follow that all men are oppressive; and to regard almost every instance of masculine insensitivity or even abuse as conscious tyranny and sadism is to oversimplify the problems between men and women. Edith Wharton had an enormous distance to cover from Mr. Ramy in 1892—a housebreaker, a dope-addict, a wife-beater, a thief, and a derelict—to human beings such as Lawrence Selden, Ethan Frome, or Newland Archer, characters who may be weak but who are so at least partially because they are almost as trapped and victimized by the patriarchy as the women they love. Wharton would never create men who equaled her women as sympathetic or attractive characters, although she did want to, as *The Fruit of the Tree* (1907) sets out to prove. But at least she could do better than the caricature Mr. Ramy.

Eight years passed before Wharton had another long manuscript to submit for publication. In 1892 *Bunner Sisters* failed to get into print, but in 1900 *The Touchstone*—quickly followed by *The Valley of Decision* in 1902 and *Sanctuary* in 1903—launched her career as a novelist. In fact, each is a flawed book. *The Touchstone* and especially *Sanctuary* are melodramatic, and the heroines in these two short novels and in *The Valley of Decision* are wooden; at first Wharton was not able to create in a novel a woman recognizably representative but at the same time sufficiently individual to avoid being simply a "type." Whereas Lily Bart in *The House of Mirth* stands for a class of women yet emerges unique and memorable, her predecessors, by comparison, are animated mannequins. Yet, the types Wharton chose to work with and the issues she worked through and beyond served as valuable experiments, mostly because they *did* fail, in the process of growth and exploration that led to Lily Bart and *The House of Mirth*. Wharton's best work, as Gary Lindberg has pointed out in *Edith Wharton and the Novel of Manners* (1975), would look deeply into the relation between the individual and society. But as Wharton's early attempts at novels show, mastering that task involved considerable trial and error.

In terms of plot her first attempt, *The Touchstone*, is an old-fashioned sort of book. Stephen Glennard, to get money to marry the woman he loves, sells love letters written to him by a famous novelist, Margaret Aubyn, now deceased. He is debilitated by secret guilt, which his wife, Alexa, intuits and finally helps him overcome by persuading him that it is not her forgiveness but the dead Margaret's that he must seek. Thus in this conventional first novel Wharton shows respect for the woman who acts as a man's moral guide. To play the role as skillfully as Alexa does requires intelligence and talent; and for the right woman, *The Touchstone* argues, that marital role can give life purpose and dignity.

Wharton's sympathies, however, lie with the woman who is not "right" for that wifely role—Margaret Aubyn, whom Glennard found too assertive, too intellectual, too unfeminine to love and marry. While the famous novelist was another man's wife, Glennard was her devoted admirer; but then, as Wharton puts it, her husband

died precisely at the moment when Glennard was beginning to criticize her. It was not that she bored him; she did what was infinitely worse—she made him feel his inferiority. The sense of mental equality had been gratifying to his raw ambition; but as his self-knowledge defined itself, his understanding of her also increased; and if man is at times indirectly flattered by the moral superiority of woman, her mental ascendancy is extenuated by no such oblique tribute to his powers. The attitude of looking up is a strain on the muscles; and it was becoming more and more Glennard's opinion that brains, in a woman, should be merely the obverse of beauty.[11]

With no choice but to accept his rejection, Margaret Aubyn languishes and dies.

The Touchstone, like the two books that would soon follow, The Valley of Decision and Sanctuary, has a number of weaknesses; but the major problem with the novel is that Wharton confuses two issues: Glennard's rejection of Margaret Aubyn before she dies and his exploitation of her after her death. On the latter there can be no debate. He was wrong to sell the novelist's letters and should assume the guilt for that violation of her trust, whether she is alive or dead. On the former, however, Wharton implies a judgment that is not reasonable. How can we blame a man for growing cool on a woman who makes him feel stupid? We can sympathize with Margaret Aubyn, who apparently was unable to be herself and at the same time remain unthreatening to Glennard; but we can also sympathize with Glennard, intellectually outmatched by Margaret and therefore in love with her only as long as there is no possibility of having to live with her. The issue of the unloved intellectual woman, in short, is fudged in The Touchstone. Wharton has Margaret fall in love with a man her subordinate in intelligence and then blames the infatuated man for deciding he does not like the relationship enough to remain in it forever. Why should he?

As if aware of how she compromised the issue in The Touchstone, Wharton two years later, in The Valley of Decision, created a man the intellectual equal of the woman he loves, and the two characters enjoy one of the few satisfying relationships in all of Wharton's fiction. Circumstances, though, remove marriage as a possibility (and thus as a problem for Wharton). Furthermore, the couple is neither American nor contemporary. They are eighteenth-century Italians.

Primarily the novel is about a nobleman, Odo, who as a young man is inspired in political idealism by Fulvia, the learned daughter of a radical scholar who teaches them both to revere the principles behind the French Revolution. The two of them fall in love and work together to bring libertarian ideals to his principality; but they fail in their efforts, and the book ends in tragedy and retrenched conservatism. Odo's subjects, manipulated by the church, do not want his new constitution. They are afraid of change. One of them murders Fulvia following a ceremony at which she is honored with a doctorate of philosophy, and the novel concludes with Odo a disillusioned and embittered man.

The Valley of Decision is boring. But it is also, and for a number of reasons, an extremely important book in Wharton's development. Quite unlike *The Touchstone,* it demanded disciplined research and analysis: Wharton had to "work at" understanding the values and hidden mechanisms of the world she fictionalized, and the result is a studious objectivity that, transferred to contemporary America, would make many of her subsequent novels successful. Moreover, in this early novel she managed to create a male protagonist for whom we can feel sympathy and admiration; Odo is a sensitive person who cares both about other people and about issues of justice and freedom. That he is not a villain or weakling and that he is capable of loving Fulvia, a remarkable woman whose intelligence and courage might threaten other men, show a breadth to Wharton's imagination that most of her previous work does not suggest. Also the novel is important because it deals overtly with political questions. Throughout her career Wharton would examine social institutions and power structures to see how they worked, whom they served, and how they affected people, especially women. This early book openly declares that interest. The long historical novel serves as a distanced proving ground, a self-conscious yet safe public initiation into the type of serious political analysis that Wharton would go on to develop more topically in her fiction about modern America.

The Valley of Decision, and this may be its most important

message, shows in addition that Edith Wharton wanted to be
a popular, even a best-selling, author. Lew Wallace's enormous success with *Ben Hur* created a large readership for
historical novels which, as James Hart explains, crested in
1894 with *The Prisoner of Zenda*, a historical romance that
"started a fad that lasted for more than a decade, for nearly
every year saw the publication of romances about an imaginary kingdom, costume pieces filled with flashing swords,
swishing cloaks, daring intrigue, and beautiful highborn
heroines."[12] Arguments criticizing Wharton for catering to
popular expectations after 1920 and thus mongering after a
lucrative audience, overlook the fact that she began her
novel-writing career by courting popular taste. She published
a historical romance in 1902, a society novel in 1905, a
problem novel with muckraking overtones in 1907, a pica-
resque satire in 1913. All were popular forms before 1920.
Clearly, although she took issue with many popular ideas and
attitudes, particularly as they pertained to women, Wharton
did not scorn popular trends in genre. In this context, her
Valley of Decision, a book replete with many of the clichés that
Hart itemizes, is simply her first obvious bid for large-scale
commercial success.

She did not succeed entirely in *The Valley of Decision*. The
novel sold well but not spectacularly, and one problem with
Wharton's historical romance is that it is intellectually over-
bearing. The book's learnedness, its extraordinary mass of
historical and geographical detail, too often buries plot; the
reader is impressed but finally numbed. Wharton's mistake
was to try to use historical romance—by definition a low-
brow genre (its goal is to make history easy to understand)—
as a means of presenting her superb intellectual credentials.
Revealingly it was that same year, 1902, that she defended
George Eliot's right to deal with complex scientific material in
her fiction. Wharton said that there was no reason why
women must limit themselves: science, politics, and history

were the domain of all intelligent adults in her opinion.[13] Perhaps the protest helps explain her burdensome show of knowledge in *The Valley of Decision*. The novelist, although she did want to be popular, did not want to be pigeonholed as a lightweight author of diverting ladies' fiction.

The Valley of Decision makes a basic statement about Edith Wharton's ambitions as a writer. She wanted to be a commercially popular writer of serious analytical fiction. The dream only deserves emphasis because it is so absolutely ordinary, and we are too often inclined to segregate Wharton from Theodore Dreiser or Margaret Deland or Gertrude Atherton or any number of other professional writers of her day who constantly worked at trying to please the public *and* themselves. If the mix did not work in *The Valley of Decision* because Wharton, unlike George Eliot in *Middlemarch*, ostentatiously made her learned matter the foreground of her book rather than its matrix, she did not repeat the mistake in *The House of Mirth*, published three years later. Political realities, economics, history, and sociology subtly shape Lily Bart's drama much as they do Dorothea Brooke's; and with *The House of Mirth* Edith Wharton finally enjoyed her first complete success: a politically sophisticated, commercially popular novel.

Two years before *The House of Mirth*, however, Wharton published *Sanctuary* (1903). It is not a good book and, as Cynthia Griffin Wolff notes, Wharton herself seems to have wished that the melodramatic novel had not appeared;[14] yet it did, and it is important because it completes the story of Wharton's early reconnoiterings as a novelist.

In *Sanctuary* Wharton did wander. It is as if she wanted to prove, after the intellectual weightiness of *The Valley of Decision*, that she was after all a writer of "mere" ladies' fiction. Louis Auchincloss summarizes the book's preposterous plot: "Kate Peyton marries a cheat and a liar in order to become the mother of a moral defective whom he might otherwise sire upon a woman less capable of raising such offspring—surely almost a parody of a Bourget theme—and . . . she contrives to keep this offspring from committing an odious fraud by radiating sympathy to him in silent Jamesian waves."[15] *Sanctuary* invites Auchincloss's sarcasm. Kate's decision to marry the scoundrel Denis Peyton in order to bear his children is ludicrous, despite Wharton's attempt to give Kate's reasoning biological justification (which reads like something out of Frank Norris): "Something had cleft the surface of self, and there welled up the mysterious primal influences, the sacrificial instincts of her sex, a passion of spiritual motherhood that made her long to fling herself between the unborn child and its fate. . . ."[16] Kate thinks to herself, "What if she, who had had so exquisite a vision of wifehood, should reconstruct from its ruins this vision of protecting maternity—if her love of her lover should be, not lost, but transformed, enlarged, into this passion of charity for his race? If she might expiate and redeem his fault by becoming a refuge [for his children] from its consequences" (p. 66). This is feminine self-sacrifice gone berserk. Kate Peyton literally surrenders her genes to an evil man for the sole purpose of creating children who will not follow in his footsteps.

In fairness to Wharton it must be said that *Sanctuary* is an unsuccessful book precisely because the author cannot support the insanely arrogant yet masochistic fantasy of female superiority that props up her plot. Although Wharton structures the story to endorse Kate's sacrifice (she does save her son from plagiarizing architectural plans), the life that she gives Kate points in the opposite direction. The subtext says that this woman, who has no identity independent of her son, has thrown her life away. She is forced to realize "that her love for her boy had come to be merely a kind of extended egotism. Love had narrowed instead of widening her, had rebuilt [walls] between herself and life. . . . It was horrible how she had come to sacrifice everything to the one passion of ambition for her boy" (pp. 109–10). Finally, when her grown son decides to submit someone else's drawings in an architectural competition, "she felt as though she had fallen by the way, spent and broken. . . . She had sacrificed her personal happiness to a fantastic ideal of duty, and it was her punishment to be left alone with her failure, outside the normal current of human strivings and regrets" (p. 157). The book's happy ending—Kate's son responds to her moral influence and abandons the fraud—tries, without much success, to erase these bitter reflections on how she has wasted her life.

In *Sanctuary* Wharton for whatever reason (to capitalize on a market? to back-off from the conspicuous intellectualism of *The Valley of Decision*? to curb personal anger?) attempts a sentimental fiction about feminine self-sacrifice and fails miserably. The book is thematically ambivalent, and it is misandrous in a way that recalls *Bunner Sisters*. Wharton's subject was woman, but her theme definitely was not the tired ideal of female self-immolation. In 1893 in "The Fullness of Life," after arguing the opposite in the unpublished *Bunner Sisters*, Wharton first attempted to endorse sentimental pieties about the beauty of self-sacrifice for women. She was not successful with the cliché in that story, no doubt because it so patently contradicted her real feelings about marriage, and after her explorations in a few more tales and then in *The Touchstone* and *Sanctuary* happily she dropped the pretense. As a personal, felt impulse, effacement of self might be compelling; as a generalized principle for feminine behavior it proved a corrupt ideal for Edith Wharton early in her career—one that she tried to assume but after *Sanctuary* was able to discard for many years. Indeed, much like William Dean Howells before her, she would grow to loathe the ideal as one major impediment to women's freedom. (Unlike Howells, however, she would also go on to live through a modern world war that, for a variety of reasons, made her change her mind on the subject after 1920.)

Choice and execution of theme create problems in almost all of Wharton's early fiction about America. *Bunner Sisters*, *The Touchstone*, and *Sanctuary* have for their premise male exploitation and conceive of it in crude, melodramatic terms: Mr. Ramy's vicious marriage of Evelina Bunner; Stephen Glennard's sale of Margaret Aubyn's letters; Denis Peyton's complicity in the suicide of his sister-in-law. Such things happen. But they are sensational, the stuff of tabloid headlines. They respond to the rough talent of an Upton Sinclair, not to the subtle analysis of Edith Wharton. In her hands they remain incredible, lurid examples of male depravity. As a result, theme, rather than being provocative in these early books, is merely angry and superficial. To write long fiction that would be as wise in its argument as it was sophisticated in its style, Edith Wharton had to work with situations that were less bizarre and she had to dispense with super-heroines: super-author Margaret Aubyn, super-wife Alexa Glennard, super-mother Kate Peyton. She did that in *The House of Mirth*, a book about an ordinary problem, marriage, and (although we may not realize it until the end of the novel) an ordinary woman: Lily Bart.

After *The Valley of Decision* in 1902 and *Sanctuary* in 1903 Wharton's novitiate was over. She had published three novels in four years and although each of them—*The Touchstone*, *The Valley of Decision*, and *Sanctuary*—had serious problems, each had strengthened her as a writer if for no other reason than by showing what she would not do best, at least at this time in her life. So with one historical romance and two melodramas behind her, early in the first decade of the twentieth century she seems to have made the decision, now that she had some experience and confidence, to try novels that penetrated rather than tried to manufacture contemporary social questions. *The Touchstone* and *Sanctuary* get worked up about extremely unusual problems; *The House of Mirth* and *The Fruit of the Tree*, although each has its sensational elements, edge closer to fundamental difficulties likely to be faced by American women early in the new century that the Woman's Building, back in 1893, had so optimistically heralded.

The New Woman

Published within two years of each other, *The House of Mirth* (1905) and *The Fruit of the Tree* (1907) are economic novels, a popular type of book in the United States at the turn of the century. In 1902 Frank Norris's *The Pit* took the Chicago Commodities Exchange for its subject. In 1904 Ellen Glasgow's *The Deliverance* examined the Reconstruction's redistribution of land and status in the rural South. In 1906 Upton Sinclair's *The Jungle* brought to light corruption and exploitation in the meat-packing industry. In keeping with the trend Wharton wrote novels attacking the commerce of marriage. Even the title of *The House of Mirth* suggests, among other things, a mercantile firm.

The two books inaugurate Wharton's career as an important social critic. In *The House of Mirth* she leaves far behind the sentimentality of *The Touchstone* and *Sanctuary* and analyzes the purpose and price of marriage for women in the American leisure class, which is to say the class envied (no matter how unrealistically) by most of the nation. The novel was an immediate best-seller, perhaps less for its attack on marriage than for its fascinating glimpse into how the very rich amuse themselves; but in any case Wharton rapidly followed her story about Lily Bart's refusal to marry with a second novel about marriage, *The Fruit of the Tree*. It revives the theme of "The Valley of Childish Things," exploring the masculine preference for the fair child-woman over her dark adult counterpart (in this novel a New Woman of exceptional appeal), and the book concludes by arguing that marriage to even the most enlightened man is, in the end, repressive. Thus, if *The House of Mirth* shows the pitfall of not marrying in a culture that demands marriage of respectable young women, *The Fruit of the Tree* shows the pitfall *of* marrying. Together, the novels stake out fully and for the first time Wharton's essential criticism of marriage as a patriarchal institution designed to aggrandize men at the expense of women.

It may be surprising to learn that Wharton herself was comparatively happy when she wrote *The House of Mirth*. Since the turn of the century, when she first started planning the novel, she had her new home in Lenox, Massachusetts, "The Mount," to enjoy and entertain friends in, and although Teddy's health was beginning to show alarming signs of deterioration, her marriage seems to have eased for the time being into a tolerable routine of housekeeping and travel, some of it shared. When she set to work in earnest on the novel in 1903, she had behind her three volumes of short stories, a book on interior design, *The Decoration of Houses* (with Ogden Codman, Jr.), and three novels. The years between 1903 and 1907 saw her go on to publish another volume of short stories, the best-seller *The House of Mirth*, the novella *Madame de Treymes*, and the potential muckraker *The Fruit of the Tree*. She had built a circle of friends which ranged from well-known personalities like Henry James to less famous people like her longtime correspondent and friend, Sara Norton; she had a publisher glad to distribute her work; she had a public eager to read it. It was the first period of sustained confidence in Edith Wharton's life as a writer, and she took for her subject the most popular, and in some ways the most controversial, issue of the day, the marriage question.

She could almost certainly be assured of an audience. The Woman Movement by the turn of the century, in addition to having yielded some socially and politically influential organizations and symbols—the National American Woman's Suffrage Association, the National Federation of Women's Clubs, the Woman's Building at the Chicago World's Fair, the Gibson Girl in the pages of *Life*—was stimulating a new literature in America. In the imaginative realm, fiction about the New Woman burgeoned: emphatically modern heroines such as Hamlin Garland's Rose of *Rose of Dutcher's Cooly* (1895) or Gertrude Atherton's Patience of *Patience Sparhawk and Her Times* (1895), or even Harold Frederic's glamorous Celia in *The Damnation of Theron Ware* (an 1896 best-seller), who illustrates her author's ambivalence on the subject, are typical of the first run of fictive New Women. After this wave of exuberance, however, came a second generation of heroines toward the turn of the century who were less magnificent than the Roses, Patiences, and Celias who continued, by the way, to populate American novels until the 1920s. The second generation were the Carrie Meebers and Edna Pontelliers and Lily Barts, troubled and troubling young women who were not always loved by their American readers (Dreiser's and Chopin's novels were not well received, and even Wharton, though *The House of Mirth* sold well, found her heroine attacked on moral grounds). Likewise there developed in discursive literature, after the first rush of lavish enthusiasm in the popular press, a serious feminist scholarship that challenged naive complacence and self-congratulation. This literature thrived in America between the end of the nineteenth century and the end of the First World War, and it consistently focused on two issues: marriage and work.[1]

The pioneers were Charlotte Perkins Gilman and Thorstein Veblen, both of whom studied the economics of marriage for women and both of whose work helps set the stage for Wharton's treatment of the subject. Although Gilman's confidence in progress clashes with Edith Wharton's pessimism, her anatomy of the connection between marriage

and femininity has much in common with Wharton's (as
Gilman's own grim story about marriage in 1899, "The Yel-
low Wallpaper," brilliantly attests). In her groundbreaking
*Women and Economics: A Study of the Economic Relation
between Men and Women as a Factor in Social Evolution*,
published in 1898, Gilman analyzes the economics of marriage and shows that the human female's lifelong dependence
on the male is neither natural—females of other species
gather their own food—nor healthy. The human system
breeds excessive "sex-distinction" which makes women, like
milch-cows artificially kept lactating, focus their entire identity on gender, to the point that even hands and feet—
prehensile and locomotive appendages—become secondary
sex characteristics: soft, dainty, and so forth. The cause of
the problem is not biology but the social fact that the human
female, merely to subsist, has had to develop exaggerated
femininity; her "economic profit comes through the power of
sex-attraction."[2] Not that woman is supported in return for
her labor in the home as wife and mother: "The women who
do the most work get the least money, and the women who
have the most money do the least work."[3] Rather, a wife, like
a horse, as Gilman puts it, labors in partnership with man but
lacks autonomy; she is fed and cared for according to her
keeper's pleasure and principles. Pleasing a man therefore
becomes woman's job in life, which means that the married
woman, viewed economically, differs very little from the prostitute; both exchange sexual service for support. It is a concept that Edith Wharton's Gus Trenor, in *The House of Mirth*,
understands only too well.

One year after *Women and Economics* appeared, Thorstein
Veblen published *The Theory of the Leisure Class: An Economic Study of Institutions* (1899). Convinced that the leisure class serves as the ideal to which all classes aspire in any
given culture—an assumption Edith Wharton obviously
shared—Veblen analyzes the leisure-class wife's role and dif-

fers from Gilman in arguing that, though wives are dependent economically on men, they do fulfill a significant function in the marital economy: that of conspicuous consumer for the male. They display his wealth, and therefore power, by spending his money while leading lives of leisure, "thereby putting in evidence his ability to sustain large pecuniary damage without impairing his superior opulence."[4]

Thus, according to Veblen, the leisure-class wife (and all her imitators) has a definite job to perform, and "it is an occupation of an ostensibly laborious kind. It takes the form, in large measure, of painstaking attention to the service of the master," which means deferring, like the rest of his servants, to his wishes and wearing his livery.[5] Like his footman, the gentleman's wife wears clothing that shows she does not need to engage in sweated labor. Indeed, her huge hats, high heels, voluminous skirts, excessively long hair, and corseted midriff all render her unfit for exertion and label her some man's costly possession. She is human chattel with an ornamental function, the prized domestic trophy whose leisure, dependence, and expenditure evidence her husband's financial prowess. For Veblen, and for Wharton, the lady of the leisure class is not an individual to be envied. She is a symbol to be studied, a totem of patriarchal power.

Edith Wharton took the title for her novel from the Bible: "The heart of the wise is in the house of mourning; The heart of fools is in the house of mirth."[6] After experimenting with a couple of names for her heroine— Rose, Julia Hurst (an unsympathetic name that brings to mind inanimate matter and the powerful Hearst syndicate that Wharton despised), she settled on Lily Bart, a name that calls up another passage from the Bible, this one from the Sermon on the Mount: "And why are you anxious about clothing? Consider the lilies of the field, how they grow; they neither toil nor spin; yet I tell you, even Solomon in all his glory was not arrayed like one of these" (Matt. 6:28; Luke 12:27). The allusion is cynical.

Lilies may not spin but they certainly toil, and toil constantly
(albeit invisibly, just like Wharton's Lily—in fact the appearance of carefreeness is one of the things that makes both
flowers and beautiful women valuable); or they die.
Moreover, there are even lilies of the field that toil and toil
constantly and still die, killed by drought, flood, frost—any
number of external disasters. Wharton's is one of those lilies.
She works hard to survive but nevertheless dies prematurely,
or more accurately is killed, blotted out. To use Lily's own
image, she is thrown out "on the rubbish heap."[7] This happens to her for one reason: she refuses to marry, an action
that not only makes her useless to the society Wharton portrays, but also, and for the reasons Gilman and Veblen outline, threatening.

When the novel opens, Lily Bart, at twenty-nine, needs a
husband. She has already netted but then let drift away several
lucrative proposals of marriage, and she does not have much
time left. With no immediate family and no inheritance to fall
back on, her only dowry is her beauty and style, and both
require enormous upkeep—gowns and accessories from
Paris and large sums of cash to wager at fashionable bridge
tables. Lily manages because her wealthy friends replenish
her wardrobe and purse to keep her among their ranks.
"Brought up to be ornamental" (p. 480), she is valuable to
them as a symbol, the Veblenesque female whose conspicuous leisure and freedom from sweated labor display her class's
superiority to ordinary economic exigencies. Her friend Lawrence Selden, also a blueblood, begins to suspect early in the
novel "that she must have cost a great deal to make, that a great
many dull and ugly people must, in some mysterious way,
have been sacrificed to produce her," and he wonders: "Was it
not possible that the material was fine, but that circumstance
had fashioned it into a futile shape?" (p. 7).

Lawrence Selden may think that Lily has been fashioned
into a futile shape (which is slightly comical coming from

him, a dilettante of sorts), but he is wrong. Part of the point of
The House of Mirth, which charts Lily's expulsion from the
leisure class—her two-year descent from favor among the
wealthy to death in the hall-bedroom of a shabby working-
class boardinghouse—is to dramatize how perfectly trained
she is for the important job society expects her to serve as
some rich man's wife.

From the first page of the novel Lily Bart is hard at work
using the skills of her trade—charm, sex appeal, solicitude—
to entertain and give pleasure to other people. Her assign-
ment is to practice the social arts, which consist of dressing
well, serving tea properly, receiving and making visits, being
a helpful and engaging houseguest, and playing bridge.
These chores create a busy work-schedule for the leisure-
class young woman; and it *is* work in Wharton's opinion,
however degrading. One need only consider Lily's meeting on
the train with Percy Gryce, a dull young bachelor worth
millions, to appreciate the talent and training that go into her
job of drawing him out. Wharton tells us that Lily "felt the
pride of a skillful operator" (p. 30). "She had the art of giving
self-confidence to the embarrassed" (p. 27). "She questioned
him intelligently, she heard him submissively. . . . He grew
eloquent under her receptive gaze" (p. 31). Lily beautifully
illustrates Veblen's observation that "the servant or wife
should not only perform certain offices and show a servile
disposition, but it is quite as imperative that they show an
acquired facility in the tactics of subservience."[8] Again, in her
encounter later with George Dorset, the wealthy husband of a
friend who wiles away her time by having affairs with other
men, among them Selden, we are told that "Lily's arts . . .
were especially adapted to soothe an uneasy egoism" (p.
206). Lily is excellent at her job. Not only has she mastered
the social arts, but she knows how to use them to soothe and
flatter the egoism of other people, particularly men, in order
to gain her own ends without appearing direct or threatening.

On the surface she perfectly embodies society's ideal of the female as decorative, subservient, dependent, and submissive; the upper-class norm of the lady as a nonassertive, docile member of society.

But only on the surface. In fact Lily has merely learned to suppress and camouflage her own impulses and ambitions. Even though she acquits herself of the social arts in which she has been so carefully bred, she transgresses other moral and social regulations with which society expects compliance. She visits Selden alone in his apartment; she gets deeply into debt; she borrows money from a married man, Gus Trenor, and is seen leaving his town house late at night; she spends time alone with another married man, Dorset, and becomes the object of rumors; she takes a job as a private secretary to the flashy, nouveau-riche Mrs. Hatch. Her behavior is nonconformist, as are her real ambitions. She has "fits of angry rebellion against fate, when she longed to drop out of the race and make an independent life for herself" (p. 61). The seal on her stationery, with its flying ship and the motto *"Beyond!,"* images her true aspiration: she wants to escape—she wants to govern her own course in life. Her problem is that she is equipped for no life except the one she leads.

The job she has been trained for is highly specialized and her skills, if she does not choose to use them as some rich man's wife, are not transferable (or at least not in any way compatible with her pride: she has the opportunity to make money as a human mannequin modeling hats in a millinery shop, but refuses the job; it is simply a vulgar variant on what she is trying to escape). All her training and hard work wasted, Lily realizes late in the novel that she is "no more than some superfine human merchandise," and admits: "I can hardly be said to have an independent existence. I was just a screw or a cog in the great machine I called life, and when I dropped out of it I found I was of no use anywhere else" (pp. 412, 498). Lily is absolutely correct. She has utility only so long as she remains in good standing within the class that produced her.

Her utility within that class is clearly spelled out by Wharton. Men go out into the commercial world to accumulate goods and money, but unless the rich man also accumulates a woman, all his money and property and power do not extend beyond the narrow mercantile world into the social realm, into the society at large. Therefore for a rich man, ownership of a woman is not a luxury, but a necessity. She is his means of disseminating Wall Street power beyond the limited masculine world of Wall Street. Hence the economics of being a woman in Lily's world amount to working as a wife, and working hard, to translate financial power into social power by displaying a particular man's wealth for him. Put simply, the man makes money on Wall Street which he then brings to Fifth Avenue for a woman to turn into social power to aggrandize him (and by association herself).

Simon Rosedale, a Jew, is in the novel precisely because he was not born into the system Wharton describes and therefore he has had to figure out how the "machine," to use Lily's term for it, works. When the novel opens he has already mastered the principles involved. He has accumulated his money on Wall Street and is busy deciding what woman to buy to give him the most prestige and power on Fifth Avenue. He proposes to Lily, frankly characterizing marriage as a smart business deal for both of them ("a plain business statement of the consequences" is how he phrases it), and tells her: "If I want a thing I'm willing to pay: I don't go up to the counter, and then wonder if the article's worth the price. I wouldn't be satisfied to entertain like the Welly Brys; I'd want something that would look more easy and natural, more as if I took it in my stride. And it takes just two things to do that, Miss Bart: money, and the right woman to spend it" (pp. 285, 283). Specifically, he tells Lily, "I want my wife to make all the other women feel small. I'd never grudge a dollar that was spent on that" (p. 284).

There is only one problem with this system. The most important cog in the machine is a human being; and what if the woman, Lily Bart, does not want to barter herself in marriage? What if she values personal freedom over security and does not want to spend her life owned and ruled by a man any more than she wants to spend it dependent on the charity of her old-fashioned aunt, Mrs. Peniston?

The answer to that question, toward which all of book 1 of *The House of Mirth* is structured, is primitive and brutal: Gus Trenor, who feels he has already bought Lily (he has lent her a large sum of money), tries to collect by attempting to rape her. The first book of Wharton's novel shows Lily's deviancy, her refusal to become the wife of Dillsworth, Gryce, Selden, or Rosedale, and ends in a sexual confrontation in which the head of the entire economic and social system, its most powerful august patriarch—a man Wharton even names Augustus—literally tries to force Lily into submission. He lures her to his town house late at night under the pretense that his wife is there, but Lily arrives to find that Judy Trenor is not even in town. Only Gus awaits her. He leads her to the darkened back parlor, where nothing but the fireplace gives off light, then tells her they are alone. She is terrified and begins to feel sick as he "pushed a chair between herself and the door. He threw himself in it, and leaned back, looking up at her. 'I'll tell you what I want: I want to know just where you and I stand. Hang it, the man who pays for the dinner is generally allowed to have a seat at the table' " (p. 233). If the mercantile language is the same as Rosedale's, the intent is not. "He rose, squaring his shoulders aggressively, and stepped toward her with a reddening brow. . . . He laughed again. 'Oh, I'm not asking for payment in kind. But there's such a thing as fair play—and interest on one's money—' " (p. 235). He touches her and his "face darkened to rage; her recoil of

abhorrence had called out the primitive man" (p. 236). Trenor stops short of his purpose only because Lily is able to
mask her terror and he therefore loses his nerve. Were she to
show some sign of "weakness"—that is, cry out or weep, Gus
would, Wharton leads us to believe, have sprung.

The encounter between Gus and Lily stands at the center of
The House of Mirth structurally and thematically. It is a
violent, ugly scene and probably the most important episode
in the book. In its perfect coalescence of predatory economics
and sexual politics, the scene explains why Lily, who works
very hard to line up prospective husbands, finally lets them all
get away from her: she does not want to be owned by any
man.

Marriage with Percy Gryce, for example, she foresees as a
"game" and knows that if she plays her game well she can
become "the one possession in which he took sufficient pride
to spend money on it" (p. 78). But by the time Lily envisions
marriage with Rosedale, she has lost enthusiasm for manipulating the role of the ornamental, supportive wife. She imagines he will be "kind in his gross, unscrupulous, rapacious
way, the way of the predatory creature with his mate" (p.
402); and the very thought evokes an image of "acquiescing
in this plan with the passiveness of a sufferer resigned to the
surgeon's touch" (p. 403). This image of terrible helpless-
ness reveals a lot about Lily's attitude toward marriage. She
refuses to marry Gryce, Dorset, and Rosedale because she
loves none of them. But behind her refusals lies a repugnance
toward a relationship in which a woman is powerless.

The same reason explains Lily's nervous rejection of Selden. She gives as her reason his relative poverty: life with him
would be an extension of the parasitical existence she hopes
to escape. He could not afford to provide the things she
requires, so it would be foolish to marry him. More significant, however, are Selden's Pygmalion impulses—his desire,
like George Darrow and Ralph Marvell after him, characters

in *The Reef* and *The Custom of the Country*, to rescue (which means change) the woman he loves. Selden finds his beloved too beautiful for the coarse world; he wants to save her; he wants to "lift Lily to a freer vision of life" (p. 257). As in the Pygmalion story, the key scene is one in which the female appears as a human statue. In Wharton's version, Selden gazes on Lily's frozen beauty as Reynolds's Mrs. Lloyd in a tableau vivant and, yielding to the "vision-making influences as completely as a child to the spell of a fairy-tale" (p. 215), decides to renew his proposal of marriage. Wharton's choice of the painting by Reynolds comments on Selden's romantic impulse, for Mrs. Lloyd, wearing a diaphanous gown, is a graceful yet voluptuous woman captured in the act of inscribing the surname Lloyd on a tree. Obviously this portrait/ tableau appeals to Selden's aesthetic sense and at the same time to his sensuality, but also and perhaps more importantly to his vanity—the real motive of Pygmalion, a storybook hero who also fell in love with a statue he envisioned bringing to a higher order of existence. No doubt Selden, the product of his upbringing and environment just as Lily is, would like to remodel his beloved in the image of his mother.

> Unfortunately, he found no way as agreeable as that practised at home; and his views of womankind in especial were tinged by the remembrance of the one woman who had given him his sense of "values." It was from her [his mother] that he inherited his detachment from the sumptuary side of life: the stoic's carelessness of material things, combined with the Epicurean's pleasure in them. Life shorn of either feeling appeared to him a diminished thing; and nowhere was the blending of the two ingredients so essential as in the character of a pretty woman. (p. 246)

This may describe an admirable image of womanhood, but it is one that Lily Bart in no way embodies. Marriage to Selden, though the two do love each other in some ways, clearly would involve what Lily fears from any prospective husband: proprietorship.

Because marriage is the vocation expected of all young women in her class, Lily's refusal to marry inevitably leads to ostracism. She is abandoned by the affluent, and she finds herself completely unable to support herself; her attempt to learn a trade, millinery, ends in dismissal; she cannot master the manual skills involved. She finds herself out on the street, like Ann Eliza Bunner, indigent. Persuaded of her own uselessness and insignificance by loneliness and poverty—the results of failure in the outer work-world—Lily decides that she must try to get back to social acceptance in the leisure class. She therefore determines to marry Rosedale and with that decision, even though the marriage never comes to pass, we see that Lily has been forced, finally, to give up all ambition for independence; the social system has triumphed. Her spirit has been crushed.

The structure of *The House of Mirth* mirrors that gradual, undramatic debilitation of Lily's spirit. Whereas, as R. W. B. Lewis has pointed out, book 1 is conventionally structured by Lily's behavior, book 2 is much more sprawling and chaotic.[9] It is so for a reason. Book 1 is tightly controlled by Lily's actions, actions that defy society's dictum that young women must marry, and therefore actions that lead relentlessly to the sexual violence of the scene between Lily and Gus Trenor at the center of Wharton's novel. The looser structure of book 2 follows the downward gyre of Lily Bart's life from the Dorsets' companion, to the Gormers' social secretary, to Mrs. Hatch's private secretary, to common labor in a millinery workshop, to death in a cheap boardinghouse. Thematically this spiral emphasizes Lily's deteriorating control over her own life. Because she refuses to marry even though she is getting older and poorer, she must accept a series of increasingly despised positions and therefore becomes increasingly ostracized and helpless. The result is her unfocused spin away from potential self-determination to complete subjugation to external control, first from people and eventually from abstract forces such as poverty and anxiety. Book 2 grows chaotic, it disintegrates structurally, to show Lily's life "in the rubbish heap" (p. 498).

The House of Mirth is the first in a series of Wharton novels to examine the dilemma of the young American woman whose objective in life is independence but whose one option is marriage. As Selden remarks in the novel's opening scene, "Isn't marriage your vocation? Isn't it what you're all brought up for?" (p. 13). The modern world may be in its twentieth century, Wharton seems to say, but the issues of marriage and work for women are still far from solved; Lily, for all her new yearnings, has no new ideas or alternatives. (She answers Selden's question, "I suppose so. What else is there?" [p. 13].) This particular heroine is, of course, the product of a very special, conservative class, which does explain her extreme inability to survive (most of Wharton's subsequent heroines will at least not die). Still her life is instructive. She sits in Selden's flat in that first scene in the novel and says, "How delicious to have a place like this all to one's self! What a miserable thing it is to be a woman" (p. 9). Why it is a miserable thing to be a woman is the subject of *The House of Mirth*, and Lily's story does not exist in isolation. It has significance for every woman in the novel: from the richest, Mrs. Charles Augustus Trenor, to the poorest, Mrs. Haffen.

Wharton has Lily's struggle touch and reflect on the lives of a hierarchy of women whose fortunes, true to Charlotte Perkins Gilman's generalization, descend the harder they work: from the leisure-class wife or daugher (Judy Trenor, Bertha Dorset, and Evie Van Osburgh), to the parvenu (Mrs. Welly Bry and Norma Hatch), to the social conservationist (Mrs. Peniston), to the social parasite (Grace Stepney), to the social manager (Carry Fisher), to a social worker (Gerty Farish), to an industrial forewoman (Miss Haines), to an office-girl (Nettie Struther), to a manual laborer (Miss Kilroy), to a charwoman (Mrs. Haffen). All of these women have one thing in common: dependence on Wall Street. Without the rich man's money and favor no woman in *The House of Mirth* could function, and the system is designed to keep women in divisive and relentless competition for that money and favor. The feud that fans out between Bertha Dorset and Lily Bart illustrates the point. When Bertha thinks Lily is trying to steal Selden, she retaliates by stealing Percy Gryce and giving him to Evie Van Osburgh. Meanwhile, Bertha's love letters to Selden are stolen by his cleaning woman, Mrs. Haffen, who sells them to Lily, who buys them with money Gus Trenor gave to her instead of to Carry Fisher, the usual beneficiary of his superfluity. Later, to camouflage another love affair and thereby preserve her lucrative marriage, Bertha libels Lily; that loss of reputation, on top of Grace Stepney's disparaging revelations, results in Mrs. Peniston's cutting Lily out of her will, which bequeaths the fortune of the late *Mr.* Peniston.

This labyrinth of exploitation and theft justifies Selden's dismay "at the cruelty of women to their kind" (p. 352), a cruelty that is not natural in Wharton's opinion. Relationships between women in this novel, as in the ones to follow, are frequently hostile. Forbidden to aggress on each other directly, or aggress on men at all, women prey on each other—stealing reputations, opportunities, male admirers —all to parlay or retain status and financial security in a world arranged by men to keep women supplicant and therefore subordinate. That women by nature feel no necessity to harm each other, indeed often quite the opposite, Wharton suggests in a number of instances involving Lily and, significantly, other women who know what it means to have to depend on oneself for one's livelihood. Carry Fisher helps Lily find employment among the second-echelon wealthy after she has been "cut" by the elite. Miss Kilroy, a fellow "work-woman" in the millinery sewing-room where Lily tries to get a new start, commiserates with Lily and cheers her with some friendly words. Nettie Struther, whom Lily met on visits to Gerty Farish's Working Girls' Club and helped out financially (ironically with Gus Trenor's money), takes Lily home with her when she finds her former benefactress sitting like a derelict on a park bench. Most loyal is Lily's cousin, Gerty. By no accident Lily runs to her and sleeps in her arms on the night she escapes Gus Trenor's assault. Gerty is at times silly and at time jealous, but she is also sisterly: she extends the same unfailing emotional support to Lily that she has for the downtrodden women she ministers to in her social work. At the beginning of *The House of Mirth* Selden escorts resplendent Lily "past sallow-faced girls in preposterous hats, and flat-chested women struggling with paper bundles and palm-leaf fans. Was it possible that she belonged to the same race?" (p. 6). Wharton answers that question in the end, yes.

Even though we never see it, Gerty's Girls' Club, where Lily meets Nettie Struther, serves as an important symbol in *The House of Mirth*. For her contemporary audience Wharton did not need to do more than refer to the club; its purpose and character would have been well known. For example, as early as 1894 her sister-in-law, Mary Cadwalader Jones, talks about Working Girls' Clubs in her chapter on "Women's Opportunities in Town and Country" in Scribner's *Woman's Book*. She explains that, happily, the days of Lady Bountiful-type philanthropy are past; in its stead is a new type of social work, free of condescension and done by women organized to act as part of a group. Typical would be settlement work, work with Girls' Friendly Societies or Y W C A 's, work with kindergartens and day nurseries, or work with Working Girls' Clubs. The clubs were places where overworked, underpaid shop-girls, typists, stenographers, and other young female laborers could congregate, make friends, and share grievances. They were, in effect, safe harbors for young women employees without friends or family in the city.

The point of alluding to Working Girls' Clubs in *The House of Mirth* is ironic. While Lily labors to survive among the extremely wealthy, some of the money that Gus Trenor tried to buy her with goes, via Gerty, to other young women laborers who are equally exploited, her "sisters" in the world of mercantile and menial labor. Wharton thus establishes in the background of Lily's drama a connection between her problem and that of lower-class women. They are bound together, as Lily's life in the millinery workshop and her statement "I have joined the working classes" (p. 468) finally show quite literally, by the common bond of economic struggle. Five years after *The House of Mirth*, in *The Lady: Studies of Certain Significant Phases of Her History* (1910), the scholar Emily Putnam observed that the leisure-class woman's "prestige is created by the existence of great numbers of less happy competitors who present to her the same hopeless problem as the stoker on the liner presents to the saloon-passenger. If the traveller is imaginative, the stoker is a burden on his mind. But after all, how are saloon-passengers to exist if the stoker does not? Similarly the lady reasons about her sisters five decks below."[10] Wharton constructs *The House of Mirth* to show the existence of these decks *and* the passageway between them. It is no accident that the last woman we know Lily sees before she dies is Nettie, and the first person to discover her death is Gerty.

The depth of Lily's tragedy becomes fully apparent shortly before her death when she sits in Nettie Struther's tenement kitchen while the young woman prepares supper and feeds the baby. "Such a vision of the solidarity of life had never before come to Lily. . . . All the men and women she knew were like atoms whirling away from each other in some wild centrifugal dance: her first glimpse of the continuity of life had come to her that evening in Nettie Struther's kitchen" (p. 516). Lily envies Nettie's maternal happiness, but even more so the relationship between a man and a woman that created her home: "it had taken two to build the nest; the man's faith as well as the woman's courage" (p. 517). Lily's image of marriage has been so necessarily class-defined in terms of conspicuous consumption that she never saw its potential to secure a bond of faith and courage between a man and woman in order to bring them into the continuity of life through parenthood. *The House of Mirth* does not idealize motherhood per se. It uses an image of motherhood to reinforce its criticism of American marriage, especially in the leisure class, which is so obsessed with producing ornamental wives that the companionate potential of the institution is missed.

Lily's final action in *The House of Mirth* shows the leisure class's complete (and appropriately absentee) victory over her desire for autonomy. She dies by her own hand but not by her conscious will: it is not really suicide. "She did not, in truth, consider the question very closely—the physical craving for sleep was her only sustained sensation" (p. 521). Ironically, Lily craves in the end the docility society has all along expected of her. She increases the dosage of sleeping medicine to achieve "the gradual cessation of the inner throb, the soft approach of passiveness . . . the sense of complete subjugation" (pp. 521–22). On a symbolic level, she is murdered by her culture; and its ghastly triumph is to make her its agent, its last enforcer of a literal and permanent passivity on Lily Bart.

That depressing victory is mitigated somewhat by Wharton's important final image of Lily. She dies totally passive, hallucinating that she cradles in her arms the infant girl-child of another woman. Literally a self-embrace, the poignance of which recalls the night she spent in Gerty's arms at the end of book 1, this image does not really imply unfulfilled motherhood; Lily has no illusion that the baby is hers. Rather, the book ends with Lily's imagining the warmth of Nettie Struther's infant flowing through her drugged, passive, dying body. Half-asleep, she "started up again, cold and

trembling with the shock: for a moment she seemed to have
lost her hold of the child. But no—she was mistaken—the
tender pressure of its body was still close to hers: the recovered warmth flowed through her once more, she yielded to
it, sank into it, and slept" (p. 523). In the arms of the ornamental, leisure-class Lily lies the working-class infant
female, whose vitality succors the dying woman. In that
union of the leisure and working classes lies a new hope—the
New Woman that Wharton would bring to mature life in her
next novel.

That novel, *The Fruit of the Tree* (1907), sets out to be a
very modern book. Wharton clearly wanted to keep the large
audience she had attracted with *The House of Mirth*, and she
picked subject matter that could compete with contemporary
best-sellers like Ellen Glasgow's *The Wheel of Life* or Upton
Sinclair's *The Jungle* (the political position of which she disliked intensely). Hildegarde Hawthorne explained at the
time, rather awkwardly it must be owned: "In her last book,
'The Fruit of the Tree,' Mrs. Wharton uses the dramatic situation in which the opposing ideas represented by labour and
capital now stand in such clear definition as the background
on which to spread the web of her plot."[11] Like its predeces-
sor, or even more so, then, *The Fruit of the Tree* is an
economic novel. It is also a problem novel that skirts in
addition with being a muckraker. The problem it examines is
euthanasia, and the muckraking it deals with involves inhuman working conditions in a mill town in western Massachusetts.

Wharton's plot is complicated. The novel's main characters
are a reform-minded industrialist, John Amherst, and a
trained surgical nurse, Justine Brent; although they marry
halfway through the story, they are simply friends when the
book opens. Justine works in the local hospital, where she
attends a man whose hand has been mangled irreparably at
the local mill; Amherst is an assistant manager at that mill.

Because he won't take bribes, Amherst is fired. But then Bessy Westmore, the young widow who inherited the mill, falls in love with him, they marry, and he becomes the manager of the whole operation. His plans for factory reform and his marriage, however, soon go sour because of Bessy; she resents the attention and money he puts into the mill. The couple therefore separates and Amherst takes a new job in South America. While he is gone, Bessy has a terrible riding accident; for weeks she lies in bed with no hope of survival, paralyzed and in agony: she is prevented from dying only by her doctor's superhuman exertions. Justine, Bessy's friend and the nurse on the case, finally countermands the doctor in secret and administers a lethal dose of morphine, at Bessy's request; and it is that act, months later, which ruins Justine's life. Discovery of the euthanasia poisons her marriage to Amherst.

Critics point out that *The Fruit of the Tree* attempts so much that it does not do justice to its separate strands, and the book as a whole does not hang together. On the one hand there is the difficult topic of euthanasia. On the other there is the story of John Amherst's desire to reform working conditions at the Westmore Mill, and Wharton's handling of this industrial setting has drawn attention. To create her town of Hanaford she toured mills in North Adams, Massachusetts, close to her home in Lenox, and the din was so overwhelming that she got details confused; readers at the time, and critics in ours, cite the fact that errors mar her depiction of mill life. [12] But in my opinion what keeps the novel from realizing its muckraking potential is not really a simple matter of the elegant author's becoming rattled by the environment she researched in North Adams. Had Edith Wharton wanted to learn exactly how a factory runs there is no doubt that she could have done so, superbly. *The Valley of Decision*, if it proved nothing else, showed that she could research material more than competently. Wharton gives a comparatively

sloppy, vague picture of factory life in *The Fruit of the Tree*
because, finally, she is only vaguely interested in industrial
reform. Mainly she is interested in the relationship between
John Amherst, the would-be reformer, and Justine Brent.
Justine is one of Wharton's warmest characterizations
(biographers frequently remark that the author put more of
herself into this character than most); and she brings together the best characteristics of the genteel woman and the
working woman as they appeared in *The House of Mirth*. Like
Lily Bart, Justine is physically attractive and responsive,
well-bred, and appreciative of tasteful surroundings (an important point with Wharton). Like Gerty Farish, she is economically self-sufficient, concerned about the poor, and loyal
to her friends' best interests even at the expense of her own.
Unlike any character in *The House of Mirth*, however, she is
in addition a thoroughly New Woman. Although she was
raised in a traditional, wealthy family and educated in Paris,
her parents died before she was twenty, leaving her without
money or means of support. Justine looked at her situation
and decided to train for a surgical nurse.

Nursing was a coming profession for women at the turn of
the century. It had only been forty years since Florence Nightingale and then in this country Clara Barton had introduced
the concept of training nurses; before that, although women
had always been expected to tend the sick, they were not
trained for the job and no respectable woman worked in a
hospital. The care of sick and dying strangers was left to
Dickensian creatures recruited from poorhouses and prisons. Crusaders like Florence Nightingale and Clara Barton
began to turn opinion around (which mainly objected to
women dealing publicly with nakedness, gore, and excre-
ment) so that by the end of the nineteenth century in America
trained nursing was a promising and in many quarters respectable occupation. As a matter of fact, between 1890 and
1900 the number of young women enrolled in training

schools in the United States multiplied elevenfold, and the number of schools more then twelvefold, and in 1896 nurses formed the American Nurses Association, which established its own journal four years later. With the advent of the first university program in nursing in 1899, American nurses by 1900 had successfully professionalized their ranks and, thus, their image.[13] Most important, perhaps, they brought about that upgrading of the profession themselves.

Nursing is also an attractive profession for a young woman like Justine because it was one of the few occupations that did not require money to enter. To become a typist or stenographer a young woman had to have enough money to attend a business college, unless she was lucky enough to have a friend or relative who could teach her the skills she needed (and could lend her a typing machine to practice on). Nursing schools, once one was admitted, provided room and board in exchange for student-labor on the hospital wards. Indeed, the set-up might look so attractive to some young women that *The Woman's Book*, in its lead chapter on "Occupations," devotes a lot of space to the profession and cautions: "Those who imagine that the chief duties of the trained nurse, whether in private or hospital practice, are to take the temperature of patients and make delicacies in the way of jellies, broths, and eggnog have but small knowledge of the real duties devolving upon the competent nurse."[14] For a sound notion of the competent nurse's routine *The Woman's Book* quotes at length from "the journal of a head nurse at the Charity Hospital, New York, quoted by Mrs. Frederic Rhinelander [Mary Cadwalader] Jones in an excellent article entitled 'The Training of a Nurse,' which appeared in *Scribner's Magazine* for November, 1890."[15] The journal entry describes a long, exhausting, typical day on the job. Wharton may have seen this article, since her sister-in-law wrote it, or she may have become interested in the nursing profession because of her own contact with nurses during the 1890s when she required medical attention for the nervous breakdowns she suffered. In any case, whatever *The Fruit of the Tree* lacks in describing factory practices it makes up in its accurate picture of nursing and the type of woman who would be drawn to it.

Justine excels at her profession because it provides an outlet for her energetic nature which, unlike Lily Bart's, has not been suppressed or perverted. For example, when her friend Bessy Amherst claims that a woman finds happiness by becoming a passive object of interest to a man, Justine remarks, "I'm not sure about that. . . . I'm sure the passive part is always the dull one: life has been a great deal more thrilling since we found out that we revolved about the sun, instead of sitting still and fancying that all the planets were dancing attendance on us."[16] Justine Brent has no desire to turn herself into a social ornament or a domestic decoration. When she begins to acclimate to leisure-class idleness while on vacation at a country house, she resolves to return to work. She thrives on physical and mental activity and the challenge of responsibility, both of which her profession disciplines and channels into useful service.

Wharton respects Justine's ambition to serve people because it is not motivated by any false ideal of feminine self-sacrifice. "Philanthropy?" Justine asks. "I'm not philanthropic. I don't think I ever felt inclined to do good in the abstract. . . . It's only that I'm so fatally interested in people that before I know it I've slipped into their skins . . . and I can't help trying to rescue myself from *their* troubles!" (p. 231). Certainly this explains her bold ethical behavior. Even though it is a breach of professional etiquette, she tells Amherst the true extent of the millhand's injury when the bosses lie to him; she takes it upon herself to write to Amherst in South America urging him to return to his

estranged wife Bessy; she administers the overdose of morphine to Bessy after the fatal accident; she tells Bessy's father, Mr. Langhope, what she has done.

Justine's self-image, like her temperament, differs greatly
from that of Lily Bart, who lingers over the Van Osburgh
wedding jewels and thinks, "they symbolized the life she
longed to lead, the life of fastidious aloofness and refinement
in which every detail should have the finish of a jewel, and the
whole form a harmonious setting to her own jewel-like rare-
ness" (*The House of Mirth*, p. 144). Whereas Lily would like
to be a finely set human jewel, Justine would like to be a bird:
"Oh, what a good life—how I should like to be a wander-bird,
and look down people's chimneys twice a year!" (pp. 301–2).
In addition to choosing a natural rather than a manufactured
image, Justine sees herself as animate, mobile, self-reliant,
and party to other people's affairs. In fact she sees herself as
she is. Active by nature and independent by choice, she is a
perfect New Woman, a person who combines culture and
refinement with self-sufficiency and social activism. Yet
when we last see this brave New Woman she is the prisoner of
a paternal, authoritarian husband.

Wharton was never able to write a happy, positive story
about the New Woman in America, and she did not fail because she was reactionary or unconcerned. Justine Brent,
like Sophy Viner after her, demonstrates the opposite. Attuned to and sympathetic with "the woman question" in her
fiction before the 1920s, Wharton was quite capable of creating ambitious, lively young women who want to be New
Women—who want to perform useful remunerated work in
the world and want to be able to choose whether or not to
marry, and to retain their individuality if they do. But the
culture, in Wharton's opinion, offers them no means of realizing their dreams. Lily Bart, Justine Brent, Mattie Silver,
Sophy Viner, Charity Royall: all end up in bondage to the past
not because Edith Wharton was cruel but because the libera-

tion, the "progress," that America boasted of for women was, in her view, a mirage. Justine can remain single and new, and be lonely; or she can enjoy the companionship of marriage, which means giving up all her independence. She *thinks* she can be both married and new, but she cannot. Marriage and the New Woman are antithetical, Wharton argues, and, twentieth-century optimism notwithstanding, it is marriage, not freedom for women, that the culture stands by.

To round out her life Justine marries John Amherst. He seems to be a man of liberal sentiments and advanced views; he respects Justine and welcomes her aid as a fellow reformer. Together, they could design and institute changes that would make life safer and more pleasant for the mill-hands and their families. And for a while Justine finds married life all that she hoped. She and her husband plan and carry out reforms, discussing them at his office and at home in the Westmore mansion, which she has managed to make less pretentious and more comfortable. Their stepdaughter, Cicely, and her grandfather, Langhope, live with the couple most of the time and provide them with the pleasures of family life from the outset. Best of all, the couple enjoys an uninhibited mental and sexual compatibility that fulfills their open and passionate natures. Then all of this happiness shatters when Amherst learns about the euthanasia.

Beyond question, Justine should have given Bessy the lethal overdose of morphine. The tragedy centers on her husband's inability to accept that action:

Her motive had been normal, sane and justifiable—completely justifiable. Her fault lay in having dared to rise above conventional restrictions, her mistake in believing that her husband could rise with her. . . . She perceived that, like many men of emancipated thought, he had remained subject to the old conventions of feeling. And he had probably never given much thought to women till he met her—had always been content to deal with them in the accepted currency of sentiment. (p. 525)

Amherst prides himself on his independence from narrow intellectual and moral views. His enlightened industrial ideals fly in the face of accepted tradition, and the maxims he values most, like Wharton herself, as her diary entries show, contend: *"La vraie morale se moque de la morale . . . We perish because we follow other men's examples . . . Socrates used to call the opinions of the many by the name of Lamioe—bugbears to frighten children . . ."* (p. 429, Wharton's ellipses and italics; cf. p. 523). Yet when Justine acts on these principles, Amherst is repelled; his emotional aversion overruled his intellectual sanction.

The stumbling block for Amherst is not the fact that the recipient of the euthanasia, Bessy, was his wife. The two were hopelessly estranged at the time of her death and he never doubts that Justine, as the nurse on the case, helped her friend die out of compassion, with no thought of personal benefit. Rather, Amherst cannot accept Justine's action because she performed it on her own initiative, out of her own sense of moral autonomy, and did not feel bound to seek his approval after the fact. Although their marriage has led him to "the blissful discovery that women can think as well as feel," and "this discovery had had the effect of making him discard his former summary conception of woman as a bundle of inconsequent impulses, and admit her at a stroke to full mental equality with her lord," it is clear that what Wharton sardonically calls "this act of manumission" does not grant woman real mental or moral independence from "her lord."[17]Justine's unforgivable offense is to have kept her own counsel. "His mind could assent—at least in the abstract—to the reasonableness of her act; but he was still unable to understand her having concealed it from him" (p. 560). That she has not concealed her act, but simply never felt it her duty to bring it up, Amherst cannot conceive. Despite his liberal views, he remains utterly convention-bound in his inability to understand that Justine does not consider herself morally accountable to him.

The partnership of their marriage turns into a dictatorship. Amherst decides for both of them that they shall never discuss the euthanasia again, and makes clear to Justine that he no longer wants to work with her on an equal basis at the mill. This cutting her out of their mutual work-world forces upon her a life of dependence, submission, and inutility, exactly the opposite of what she married for. She responds to this exclusion by trying to reach him sexually. She hopes to reestablish their closeness, and "for a few days she and Amherst lost themselves in this self-evoked cloud of passion" (p. 533). Of course this fails in the long run to revive their former intimacy, which was based on a "free comradery of mind" (p. 459), and Justine has to accept their changed relationship.

The conclusion of the novel gets to the root of the issue. Fourteen months have passed: Justine attends the dedication of the Westmore Mill gymnasium, which Amherst eloquently and erroneously credits to his dead first wife, Bessy, who, out of spite for his spending her money on industrial and social reforms, actually had the gymnasium designed for her personal use. As Amherst eulogizes a Bessy who never existed,

a wave of anger swept over Justine at this last derisive stroke of fate. It was grotesque and pitiable that a man like Amherst should create out of his regrets a being who had never existed, and then ascribe to her feelings and actions of which the real woman had again and again proved herself incapable!

Ah, no, Justine had suffered enough—but to have this imaginary Bessy called from the grave, dressed in a semblance of self-devotion and idealism, to see her petty impulses of vindictiveness disguised as the motions of a lofty spirit—it was as though her small malicious ghost had devised this way of punishing the wife who had taken her place!

Justine had suffered enough—suffered deliberately and unstint-
ingly, paying the full price of her error, not seeking to evade its least
consequence. But no sane judgment could ask her to sit quiet under
this last hallucination. What! This unreal woman, this phantom that
Amherst's uneasy imagination had evoked, was to come between
himself and her, to supplant her first as his wife, and then as his
fellow-worker? (pp. 628–29)

As Justine sees it, Amherst has gone mad. As Wharton sees
it, he has simply gone ordinary.

Bessy Amherst is the adorable blonde from "The Valley of
Childish Things" brought to life ten years later in a realistic
drama about modern American experience. She is the precious child-woman preferred by men and therefore valued by
the culture over her adventurous adult sister, in this case
Justine. And she is content, in fact delighted, with her own
arrestment. Although twenty-four years old, widowed, and a
mother by the time she meets John Amherst in the early
1900s, when the novel opens, Bessy Westmore expects people to pamper her like a child. Her first husband "watched
over her as if she were a baby" (p. 211), and she asks only to
remain sheltered and indulged. She "forms all of her opinions
emotionally" (p. 87); and she has absolutely no interest in
the mill that her first husband, for some unknown reason,
willed to her management. She is, in short, both ignorant and
spoiled, which, as the family friend and Wharton's spokes-
woman Mrs. Ansell explains, makes her typical: "She [is]
one of the most harrowing victims of the plan of bringing up
our girls in the double bondage of expediency and unreality,
corrupting their bodies with luxury and their brains with
sentiment, and leaving them to reconcile the two as best they
can, or lose their souls in the attempt" (p. 281). Bessy's
father and friends assume she should devote her life to entertaining herself and others, and she agrees. Their expectations are easy and pleasant to meet. When her sybaritic
father, to amuse family friends, sarcastically says to his

grown daughter "Apply yourself, Bessy. Bring your masterful intellect to bear on the industrial problem" (p. 36), she displays no embarrassment or indignation. She shares his view of her as an incompetent adult but a perfectly darling child.

Blake Nevius correctly describes Bessy as "a composite portrait of everything that Edith Wharton disliked in her own sex."[18] Even more important than Wharton's aversion is her analysis of how a Bessy Westmore comes to be—for which we need look no further than her father, Mr. Langhope, who encourages her frivolity and denigrates her ability to think or act maturely. Significantly, in the novels through *The Age of Innocence* (1920), only Wharton's three least admirable heroines—Bessy Westmore, Undine Spragg, and May Welland—have living fathers, and it is no accident that those fathers are completely pleased with their limited daughters. For these paternal opinions symbolize on the personal level the patriarchal structure of American society, which Wharton shows is the source of woman's problems. In *The Fruit of the Tree*, for example, John Amherst in his concluding hallucination about Bessy merely comes around to the conventional way of looking at things: he does not want a wife like Justine who has an independent, adult sense of herself, personally and professionally. He wants a little-girl wife, a doll, an angel—what Hildegarde Hawthorne, one year after *The Fruit of the Tree*, dubs "the angel-fiend-chattel-toy notion" of woman;[19] and if life does not provide such a creature, his imagination will. She is essential to his sense of well-being as a man.

Patriarchal power, personified in *The Fruit of the Tree* by the deceptively innocuous Mr. Langhope, is the antagonist that stunts Bessy's growth, prohibits Justine from finding equality in marriage, and undermines Amherst's desire for revolutionary industrial improvements. In fact, criticism of patriarchal attitudes unifies this novel, which is too long and sprawling but is not nearly so disorganized or incoherent conceptually as critics have charged. Wharton's disparate domestic and industrial issues coalesce in the book's three concluding events: Amherst's assertion of authority over his wife Justine, his deluded memorialization of the child-woman Bessy, and his retreat from radical reform (the gymnasium will display the managers' benevolence rather than fundamentally improve the workers' lot). First in Langhope and then, sadly, in John Amherst, masculine egotism on all levels—personal, social, and economic—emerges as the problem Wharton attacks in *The Fruit of the Tree*.

Even though *The House of Mirth* was an enormously popular book, readers and reviewers did take Wharton to task for creating such a weak hero in Lawrence Selden. She herself had to admit that he was "a negative hero."[20] So in this next novel, she promised Scribner's that she would create "a very strong man."[21] She did. John Amherst is a warm, virile, high-principled and, finally, utterly tradition-bound hero. Compared with other Wharton men, he is somewhat sympathetic; he is a man of passion and action and for a long time he fights the anger and fear he comes to feel about Justine's autonomy. He is not a caricature or villain like some of Wharton's earlier men. Nevertheless he epitomizes the deep resistance to the idea of equality that she saw among even the most progressive American men. He plays at change, in both the industrial and the domestic worlds, but in the end prefers a world unchanged. When Bessy was alive he found her immaturity oppressive; when she is dead he can create a romantic, old-fashioned image of her that suits his fancy, and he prefers that image to the living, modern woman at his side. He would rather live with a ghost than with Justine.

Only late in the composition of the novel did Wharton decide on the title *The Fruit of the Tree*. For the many months that she thought about and worked on the book she called it simply "Justine Brent." The working title says everything about the author's allegiance in the book. She would create few other characters as splendid as Justine Brent, or as betrayed. For Wharton's New Woman, the fruit of the tree of marriage is bitter, indeed.

Love

Between the publication of *The Fruit of the Tree* in 1907 and *Ethan Frome* in 1911, Edith Wharton fell into, and what is more important, out of love. The experience was in many ways exhilarating for her personally; at the age of forty-five she came to know for the first time her own erotic potential and she discovered what it means to be so obsessed with another human being that one's former sense of reality, in this case her life as a writer, seems strange, even pointless. Not that she was unable to write at all during the three years that her affair with Morton Fullerton lasted: she continued to write short stories, she kept journals, one ordinary and the other a private diary addressed to her lover, and she wrote poetry. Also she tried to write long fiction. She started *The Custom of the Country*, which would finally appear in 1913. But she found herself unable to complete any novel for several years after her relationship with Fullerton began in 1907.

They met in the spring, becoming lovers probably sometime in the autumn. That same autumn *The Fruit of the Tree* went to press, and it was not until four years later that Wharton had another piece of long fiction for her publisher. The piece, *Ethan Frome*, is not a novel and not even all that long. Nevertheless its publication marked the beginning of an awesomely creative period for Wharton. In 1911 there was *Ethan Frome*, in 1912 *The Reef*, in 1913 *The Custom of the Country*. After four years of false starts and comparatively mediocre output, she once again had, beginning in 1911, a lot to say.

What is most striking is how little, finally, the affair changed Edith Wharton's argument. It did give her new respect for erotic motivation, which makes characters like Anna Leath and Sophy Viner, Charity Royall and Ellen Olenska more complicated and therefore more real, psychologically, than Lily Bart or Justine Brent. Analytically, however, it only deepened her developing argument with America. Despite the four-year break (a significant gap for a novelist as prolific as Wharton), Edith Wharton picked up almost where she left off in terms of her realistic social criticism: *The House of Mirth* and *The Fruit of The Tree* stand in a direct line with *Ethan Frome* and *The Reef* and *The Custom of the Country*. All five study work and marriage as the key problems affecting women.

Where *Ethan Frome* and *The Reef* deepen the argument, and the depth gained is considerable, is in taking fully into account the idea of love. In *The House of Mirth* love is barely an issue. In *The Fruit of the Tree* it is secondary. But in *Ethan Frome* and *The Reef*, love as we have been taught to expect it, as it is dreamed of for us in our fairy tales with their eternally happy endings, is Wharton's subject; and her verdict in both books is simple and harsh. She argues that until fairy-tale notions about romance and marriage are relinquished—which, given their psychological tenacity and political utility, seems unlikely in her view to happen—equality between the sexes, and thus the full emancipation of women, rich or poor, "new" or old-fashioned, will not come to pass.

Her own experience probably contributed to the conclusion. Her marriage to Teddy by 1907 was effectively over: it would be six more years and many more quarrels before their divorce, but whatever bonds may have tenuously held them together in their first years of marriage by now were completely severed. Intellectually and sexually they shared nothing. Against this situation, in her middle forties, Edith Wharton met Morton Fullerton, a handsome, interesting

American a few years her junior, and fell wildly, adolescently in love. They lived near each other in Paris and exchanged love notes that she made a little ritual out of reading each morning; she slaved over her love diary, titled "The Life Apart," which she was writing for him (and for her biographers as well, it is important to add—Wharton was hardly unself-conscious about this period in her life); she poured her creative energies into poetry, with the result that she produced some very bad verse, the worst being "Ogrin the Hermit," but also at least one very good poem, "Terminus."

Most of this personal love-literature is highly conventional and self-absorbed; in it Edith Wharton watches herself in love. She had long feared never knowing what passion was like. As she told her journal in 1908, when her relationship with Fullerton was young and the two of them were disappointed in their plan to spend a day together in the country, "I have never in my life known what it was to be happy (as a woman knows happiness) even for a single hour—now at least I shall be happy for a whole day, talking *à coeur ouvert*, saying for once what I feel and *all that I feel*, as other women do. *Ah, pauvre âme close! Y ai-je vraiment cru un seul instant? Non, je savais trop bien que quand il s'agit de moi les Erynnies ne dorment, jamais, hélas . . .*" [Ah, poor shut-in soul! Did I really believe in it for an instant? No, I knew only too well that when it comes to me, the Furies never sleep, alas.][1] With Morton Fullerton, for three years, Edith Wharton had the love affair that allowed her to feel and behave, so she imagined, "as other women do."

If Wharton's personal love-literature is conventional, even hackneyed, it is probably because the conventional, the standard experience is in many ways what she was looking for, and got, perhaps because she picked the perfect person to give it to her. Morton Fullerton practically made a career out of having affairs. When he started up with Edith Wharton he was being blackmailed by one woman with whom he had been sexually involved; at the same time he was informally engaged to marry his cousin, a woman half his age who had grown up believing herself to be his sister. Melodrama is not an extravagant term to describe Wharton's love affair with Fullerton, which for three years combined the usual stress (and excitement) of secrecy, with the novel ingredients of blackmail (from which Wharton helped Fullerton extricate himself), peripheral "incest," and belles-lettres pulse-taking.

They amicably parted as lovers (remaining friends) probably sometime in 1910. Fullerton's young cousin married someone else, leaving him restless and prompting him to change a number of relationships in his life, including the one with Edith Wharton. She in her turn, not to be too blunt, had also by 1910 gotten what she wanted out of the liaison and, as Lewis puts it, she began to take "a fresh and clear-eyed look at her lover." What she seems to have seen, in addition to Fullerton's glaring shortcomings, were her own delusions. Again to rely on Lewis, "By the summer of 1910, Morton Fullerton was no longer for Edith the man she had once dreamed of." Fullerton "was still—undependable, weak, and irresistibly attractive—the man she had loved and who had loved her. But there was to be no further intimate commerce between them."[2] Once she was able to separate the man from the dream, Edith Wharton's romance, her splendid love affair, no longer held her charmed.

Ethan Frome and *The Reef*, both written shortly after the affair with Fullerton, bring to Wharton's developing argument what she now understood about romantic love. Specifically they study fairy-tale fantasies of romantic rescue and escape. The topic was not utterly new to Wharton. In addition to early short stories that treated love as an illusory means of escape from personal unhappiness (some of the ghost and horror stories particularly evoke fairy tales in their gothic treatment of the subject), *The House of Mirth* is itself an inverted Cinderella story—the heroine going from riches to rags instead of

the other way around—and *The Fruit of the Tree* in its largest
outline reverses the Sleeping Beauty myth: Justine starts out
wide awake and ends up in a superimposed state of mental
and physical paralysis. Wharton liked to say that fairy tales
did not have much effect on her as a child, that she was more
influenced by the classics. That may be so (though the evidence points to their both being influential). In any case, she,
like Fitzgerald after her, found fairy tales very important to
what she had to say as an adult.

In *The House of Mirth*, for instance, she describes leisure-class reaction to a bad season on Wall Street:

> Fashion sulked in its country-houses, or came to town incognito,
> general entertainments were discountenanced, and informality and
> short dinners became the fashion.
>
> But society, amused for a while at playing Cinderella, soon
> wearied of the hearthside role, and welcomed the Fairy Godmother
> in the shape of any magician powerful enough to turn the shrunken
> pumpkin back again into the golden coach. . . . According to Wall
> Street rumors, Welly Bry and Rosedale had found the secret of
> performing this miracle.[3]

The Cinderella/Wall Street connection here is casual and
strictly mercenary; in *The House of Mirth* Wharton had not
yet arrived at the point in her own thinking where she could
fully appreciate and communicate the ways in which traditional fantasies of love underpin the marital economy. In *The
Fruit of the Tree* she begins to be aware of the process.
Justine's decision to marry proves disastrous because John
Amherst, for all his attempts to deny it, is tied to traditional
economic and romantic points of view which coalesce and
preclude equality of the sexes. But full exploration of the
connection between fairy-tale love and the sexual politic did
not come until *Ethan Frome* and *The Reef*.

They are unlikely companion-pieces. Whereas *Ethan
Frome* is very short and is set in impoverished rural Massachusetts, *The Reef* is a full-sized novel and is set in Paris,

the château country, and London. *Ethan Frome* is about simple people and has a straightforward narrative frame; *The Reef* is about sophisticated people and has a subtly complicated double narrative point of view; and while *Ethan Frome* invites allegorical interpretation, *The Reef* seems entirely realistic. Labeled derivatively, *Ethan Frome* is Hawthornian; *The Reef*, Jamesian.

Yet thematically these two books form a closer couple than almost any other books in Wharton's canon. Published within a year of each other, they approach "love" first from a male perspective and then from a female one, and fairy-tale visions dominate both books. Ethan dreams of marrying virginal Mattie Silver and heading West to a new place and a new life. In *The Reef* Sophy Viner, although opposed to marriage in general, plans to marry Owen Leath because his princely wealth can make her dream of financial freedom come true. Meanwhile the more conventional Anna Leath, who never questions the institution of marriage, believes that in becoming Mrs. George Darrow she will awaken to the full awareness of life that she missed in her first, loveless marriage. None of these dreams survives reality, and Wharton's moral is the same in both books: fairy-tale visions of love and marriage imprison rather than liberate men and women.

Although finally highly realistic both in its liberal social criticism and its more sweeping psychological implications, *Ethan Frome* is designed to read like a fairy tale. It draws on archetypes of the genre—the witch, the silvery maiden, the honest woodcutter—and brings them to life in the landscape and social structure of rural New England. To tell the story Wharton introduces an unnamed, educated city-dweller, who has had to piece the narrative together; all he can offer about Ethan, he announces at the end of his preface, is:

this vision of his story ....
....
....[4]

Short ellipses often appear in Wharton's fiction, but this ellipsis is excessive, and it exists to help establish genre. It trails off for three printed lines to emphasize that, while Ethan's story will appear real and we can believe that the tragedy did happen, the version here is a fabrication. It is an imagined reconstruction of events organized in part out of shared oral material and shaped for us into one of many possible narratives. As the narrator says in his opening statement: "I had the story bit by bit, from various people, and, as generally happens in such cases, each time it was a different story" (p. 3). This tale, in other words, belongs to a community of people (ourselves now included) and has many variants. Also important is Wharton's selection of the word "vision." Not a documentary term, "vision" prepares us for the fact that Ethan's story, with its vivid use of inherited symbols and character types, will seem a romance or fairy tale.

Wharton's plot, as in most fairy stories, is simple. After seven miserable years married to sickly Zeena, a woman seven years his senior, Ethan Frome (who is twenty-eight) falls in love with twenty-one-year-old Mattie Silver. She is the daughter of Zeena's cousin and works as the childless couple's live-in "girl." When Zeena banishes Mattie because she knows that Ethan and the girl have fallen in love, the young lovers try to kill themselves by sledding down a treacherous incline into an ancient elm. The suicide attempt fails, leaving Ethan lame and Mattie a helpless invalid. The narrator reconstructs this story when he visits Starkfield twenty-four years after the event; Ethan is fifty-two and the three principals are living together, Zeena taking care of Mattie and Ethan supporting them both.

Although the pattern is very subtly established, the numbers that accumulate in Wharton's story bring to mind natural cycles: fifty-two (the weeks of the year); twenty-four (the hours of the day and a multiple of the months of the year); seven (the days of the week) with its echoes in the multiples twenty-one, twenty-eight, thirty-five; three (among other things, morning, afternoon, night). The implication here of generation and natural order ironically underlines Wharton's awful donnée. Expressed figuratively: in the frozen unyielding world of Ethan Frome, there is no generative natural order; there is no mother earth. There is only her nightmare reverse image, the witch, figured in Zeena Frome.[5]

Specifically, a network of imagery and event in *Ethan Frome* calls up the fairy tale *Snow-White*. The frozen landscape, the emphasis on sevens, the physical appearance of Mattie Silver (black hair, red cheeks, white skin), her persecution by witchlike Zeena (an older woman who takes the girl in when her mother dies and thus serves as a stepmother to her), Mattie's role as housekeeper: all have obvious parallels in the traditional fairy tale about a little girl whose jealous stepmother tries to keep her from maturing into a healthy, marriageable young woman. Although Wharton is not imitating this well-known fairy tale—rather, she draws on familiar elements of *Snow-White* as touchstones for a new, original fairy tale—still, for many readers, without their even realizing it, the implicit contrast between Zeena's victory in *Ethan Frome* and the stepmother's defeat in *Snow-White* no doubt contributes to the terror of Wharton's story. Most fairy tales reassure by teaching that witches lose in the end. Children and heroines (Snow-Whites) do not remain the victims of ogres. Someone saves them. Here is part of the horror of *Ethan Frome*: Wharton's modern fairy tale for adults, while true to traditional models in the way it teaches a moral about "real" life at the same time that it addresses elemental fears (e.g., the fear of death, the fear of being abandoned), does not conform to the genre's typical denouement. The lovers do not live happily ever after. The witch wins.

Zeena's face alone would type her as a witch. Sallow-complexioned and old at thirty-five, her bloodless countenance is composed of high protruding cheekbones, lashless

Zeena Witch

lids over piercing eyes, thin colorless hair, and a mesh of minute vertical lines between her gaunt nose and granite chin. Black calico, with a brown shawl in winter, makes up her ordinary daytime wear, and her muffled body is as fleshless as her face. Late one night Ethan and Mattie return from a church dance to the dreary house where a "dead cucumber-vine dangled from the porch like the crape streamer tied to the door for a death" (p. 56). They are met by Zeena: "Against the dark background of the kitchen she stood up tall and angular, one hand drawing a quilted counterpane to her flat breast, while the other held a lamp. The light, on a level with her chin, drew out of the darkness her puckered throat and the projecting wrist of the hand that clutched the quilt, and deepened fantastically the hollows and prominences of her high-boned face" (p. 58). Confronting the youthful couple at midnight in her kitchen, "which had the deadly chill of a vault" (p. 58), Ethan's spectral wife, complete with stealthy, destructive cat, appears the perfect witch of nursery lore.

Mattie Silver, in contrast, seems a fairy maiden, a princess of nature in Ethan's eyes. Her expressive face changes "like a wheat-field under a summer breeze" (p. 98), and her voice reminds him of "a rustling covert leading to enchanted glades" (p. 100). When she sews, her hands flutter like birds building a nest; when she cries, her eyelashes feel like butterflies. Especially intoxicating is her luxuriant dark hair, which curls like the tendrils on a wildflower and is "soft yet springy, like certain mosses on warm slopes" (p. 158). By candlelight her hair looks "like a drift of mist on the moon" (p. 105). Simone de Beauvoir, quoting Michel Carrouges, provides in general terms a nearly perfect description of Mattie's psychomythic significance for Ethan: "Woman is not the useless replica of man, but rather the enchanted place where the living alliance between man and nature is brought about. If she should disappear, men would be alone, strangers lacking passports in an icy world. She is the earth itself raised to life's summit, the earth become sensitive and joyous; and without her, for man the earth is mute and dead."[6] Zeena's colors are those of the dead earth—black, grey, brown; Mattie's are blood red and snowy white. She sleeps under a red and white quilt, wears a crimson ribbon and a cherry red "fascinator," and has rosy lips and a quick blush. A vision of her face lingers with Ethan one morning: "It was part of the sun's red and of the pure glitter on the snow" (p. 62). Passion and purity mingle in Ethan's image of Mattie, making her more valuable to him (but no more attainable) than the precious metal her last name specifies.

The imagery Ethan associates with Mattie Silver is frankly sexual: visions of secret natural glens and nooks, lush dainty vegetation with dewy tendrils, mysterious mists. And his imagination turns to nature and the fairy world because the desired sexual experience is for him bound up in a masculine fantasy of possessing woman like some secret place the explorer dreams of claiming for himself. In one of the book's many sexual images anticipating the near-fatal sledding accident, Ethan calms Mattie, who is distraught because the red glass pickle dish (one of the story's obvious symbols) which she borrowed from Zeena's pitiful hoard of unused wedding gifts has gotten broken during their intimate supper. "His soul swelled with pride as he saw how his tone subdued her. . . . Except when he was steering a big log down the mountain to his mill he had never known such a thrilling sense of mastery" (p. 94). But Ethan is an unsophisticated and conscientious man; he does not want to "ruin" Mattie, nor spoil his romantic fantasy by turning their relationship into a furtive backstairs affair. Therefore he never makes love to her. Instead he dreams of getting a divorce from Zeena and marrying Mattie. He remembers a couple like themselves who did just that, moved to the West and now "had a little girl with fair curls, who wore a gold locket and was dressed like a princess" (p. 143). But the fairy tale Ethan lives, in contrast to the one he fantasizes, has a barren conclusion.

Hurting young people and depriving them of hope and joy is the fairy-tale witch's job, and Zeena does not shirk the task. She constantly finds fault with Mattie, and for seven years she has tortured her youthful husband with whining complaints about her various ailments. She even haunts Ethan. Her ugly visage takes fleeting possession of Mattie's on the blissful evening the lovers play house together, and her name, like a hex, throws "a chill between them" (p. 90). Nor will her loyal cat give them peace. The sly beast acts as Zeena's stand-in, leaping out of her rocker and setting it in eerie motion during the romantic supper the couple enjoys in her absence. In the middle of the supper the animal knocks Zeena's prized pickle dish to the floor and thus guarantees Mattie's banishment, which in turn precipitates the lovers' suicide attempt and the fairy tale's macabre denouement.

The ghastly conclusion Ethan must live with is worse than if Mattie had gone away, married someone else, or even died. The suicide attempt transforms Mattie into a mirror image of Zeena. The narrator enters the Frome house late one winter night twenty-four years after Mattie and Ethan tried to kill themselves, and he can barely tell the two women apart. The girl of Ethan's dreams now sits droning in a chair "which looked like a soiled relic of luxury" (p. 188). "Her hair was as gray as her companion's, her face as bloodless and shrivelled . . . with swarthy shadows sharpening the nose and hollowing the temples. . . . Her dark eyes had the bright witch-like stare that disease of the spine sometimes gives" (pp. 187–88).

The end of *Ethan Frome* images Zeena Frome and Mattie Silver not as two individual and entirely opposite female figures but as two virtually indistinguishable examples of one type of woman: in fairy-tale terms, the witch; in social mythology, the shrew. Mattie, in effect, has become Zeena. Shocking as that replicate image may at first seem, it has been prepared for throughout the story. Mattie and Zeena are related by blood. They live in the same house and wait on the same man, and they came to that man's house for the same purpose: to take the place of an infirm old woman (Zeena takes over for Ethan's mother, Mattie for his wife). The two women, viewed symbolically, do not contrast with each other as Justine Brent and Bessy Amherst do in *The Fruit of the Tree* nor amplify each other as Anna Leath and Sophy Viner will in *The Reef*; rather, one follows the other, walks down her road. Mattie comes to live in Zeena's house, falls in love with Zeena's husband, makes friends with Zeena's cat, tends Zeena's plants, breaks Zeena's wedding dish. She greets Ethan from Zeena's kitchen door, standing "just as Zeena had stood, a lifted lamp in her hand, against the black background of the kitchen" (p. 87). It is Zeena's terrible face that obscures Ethan's perception of Mattie when the young woman rocks in the old woman's chair on the evening they spend together, and the same hideous apparition blinds Ethan just before he and Mattie crash their sled into the tree. Zeena's identity and fate stalk Mattie until, in the end, she too becomes a witch, a miserable gnarled old woman.

As a fairy story, *Ethan Frome* terrifies because it ends askew. Incredibly, the witch triumphs. Mattie Silver becomes Zeena's double rather than Ethan's complement.

Edith Wharton said of *Ethan Frome*, "It was the first subject I had ever approached with full confidence in its value, for my own purpose, and a relative faith in my power to render at least a part of what I saw in it."[7] Her critics have not been as confident about what the story means—or *if* it means; Lionel Trilling, for example, has stated outright (and with evident irritation): "It presents no moral issue at all."[8] But as is sometimes the case, a much earlier critic did grasp Wharton's purpose. In *Voices of Tomorrow: Critical Studies of the New*

Spirit in Literature, published in 1913 (just two years after *Ethan Frome*), Edwin Bjorkman declares of the painfulness of Wharton's story:

"This one redeeming factor asserts itself subtly throughout the book, though Mrs. Wharton never refers to it in plain words. It is this: that, after all, the tragedy unveiled to us is social rather than personal. . . . If it had no social side, if it implied only what it brought of suffering and sorrow to the partakers in it, then we could do little but cry out in self-protective impatience: "Sweep off the shambles and let us pass on!" . . . Ethan and Matt and Zeena [are not presented] as individual sufferers. They become instead embodiments of large groups and whole strata; and the dominant thought left behind by the book is not concerned with the awfulness of human existence, but with the social loss involved in such wasting of human lives.

Bjorkman begins his next paragraph emphatically: "*Ethan Frome* is to me above all else a judgment on that system which fails to redeem such villages as Mrs. Wharton's Starkfield."[9]

Wharton's subsequent critics have not matched for passion or accuracy this early critical appraisal, and perhaps the problem has to do with our forgetting what life was like for many people, and particularly women, in rural America before the First World War. Wharton's usual subject was the upper- or upper-middle-class woman. Given her own station in life, she naturally understood her own type of situation best. Nevertheless, as early as her first published fiction, "Mrs. Manstey's View" in 1891, and *Bunner Sisters* a year later, Edith Wharton showed a desire to deal with the problems of poor women. One could argue that some of her attempts are inept, marred by condescension and even snobbishness; but the charge cannot be leveled at *Ethan Frome*. In it, as in *Summer* six year later, Edith Wharton's sympathies are fully engaged, and the moral she argues is clean and true.

That moral—Wharton's social criticism—emerges directly from her fairy tale. *Ethan Frome* maintains that witches are real. There are women whose occupation in life consists of making other people unhappy. *Ethan Frome* includes three. Ethan's mother, housebound and isolated for years on a failing farm, lived out her life an insane, wizened creature peering out her window for passersby who never came and listening for voices that only she could hear. Her frightening silence oppressed Ethan until Zeena joined the household to care for her. But then Zeena too fell silent. Ethan

recalled his mother's growing taciturnity, and wondered if Zeena were also turning "queer." Women did, he knew. Zeena, who had at her fingers' ends the pathological chart of the whole region, had cited many cases of the kind while she was nursing his mother; and he himself knew of certain lonely farm-houses in the neighbourhood where stricken creatures pined, and of others where sudden tragedy had come of their presence. At times, looking at Zeena's shut face, he felt the chill of such forebodings. At other times her silence seemed deliberately assumed to conceal far-reaching intentions, mysterious conclusions drawn from suspicions and resentments impossible to guess. (pp. 78–79)

Zeena's hypochondria, her frigidity, her taciturnity broken only by querulous nagging, her drab appearance—these make her an unsympathetic character. They also make her a typically "queer" woman of the region, a twisted human being produced by poverty and isolation and deadening routine. (She gives the housework to Mattie, and why not? Few jobs are more lonely or monotonous, plus the girl provides another presence in the vacant house and one on whom Zeena can vent her frustrations.) Mattie Silver is merely spared the gradual disintegration into queerness that Ethan has witnessed in Zeena and his mother. The accident, like magic, swiftly transforms the girl into a whining burdensome hag.

In reality, Mattie had no future to lose. Ethan asks for assurance that she does not want to leave the farm, and "he had to stoop his head to catch her stifled whisper: 'Where'd I go, if I did?' " (p. 54). There is nowhere for her to go. She has no immediate family and no salable skills; all she can do is trim a hat, recite one poem, and play a couple of tunes on the piano. She tried stenography and bookkeeping, both of which exhausted her, and working on her feet all day as a clerk in a department store did not bring her strength back. As Anna Garlin Spencer, Edith Wharton's contemporary, points out in a study published one year after *Ethan Frome*, laws to protect the health of women workers existed but were inadequate and seldom enforced. In *Woman's Share in Social Culture* (1912) she explains that even young women who worked only during the unmarried years between fourteen and twenty often lost their health permanently. "The fact is that because young women must all work for pay between their school life and their marriage in the case of the poverty-bound, the poorest-paid and many of the hardest and most health-destroying of employments are given to them as a monopoly." For instance:

in the canning factories 2,400 rapid and regular motions a day in tin-cutting for the girls employed. . . . In the confectionery business, 3,000 chocolates "dipped" every day at a fever heat of energy. In the cracker-making trade, the girls standing or walking [all day] not six feet from the ovens. . . . In the garment trades the sewing machines speeded to almost incredible limits, the unshaded electric bulbs and the swift motion of the needle giving early "eye-blur" and nerve strain. . . . In department stores . . . where five or six hundred girls are employed nineteen to thirty seats may be provided; but to use even these may cost the girl her position. [10]

The Woman's Book, more than a decade and a half earlier, had pointed out exactly the same abuse:

Now that some laws exist for the protection of shop-girls an attempt is made to see that they are enforced. Violations are frequently discovered. In one large shop where the law has been obeyed to the extent of putting in the one seat required for every six girls, a fine was imposed upon any girl found sitting on it! [11]

Mattie's physical inability to hold onto her job as a department-store girl is realistic. And factory work would be no better, as Edith Wharton knew from firsthand observation because she had toured industrial mills in North Adams, Massachusetts, early in the century in her research for *The Fruit of the Tree*.

Ethan thinks of Mattie "setting out alone to renew the weary quest for work. . . . What chance had she, inexperienced and untrained, among the million bread-seekers of the cities? There came back to him miserable tales he had heard at Worcester, and the faces of girls whose lives had begun as hopefully as Mattie's. . . ." (p. 133; final ellipsis Wharton's). Mattie's prospects are grim. She can work in a factory and lose her health; she can become a prostitute and lose her self-dignity as well; she can marry a farmer and lose her mind. Or she can be crushed in a sledding accident and lose all three at once. It makes no difference. Poverty, premature old age, and shattered dreams comprise her inevitable reward no matter what she does. The fact that Wharton cripples Mattie, but will not let her die, reflects not the author's but the culture's cruelty. Like Lily Bart at the opposite end of the social scale, Mattie Silver has not been prepared for an economically independent life. The system is designed to keep her a parasite or drudge, or both.

Edith Wharton's sympathy goes out to Ethan Frome. Poverty and a succession of insane, dependent women prohibit his ever having the liberty to follow his aspirations. Naturally he longs "for change and freedom" (p. 55), fantasizes Zeena's death, and sees in Mattie the incarnation of his repressed dreams. Any man in his place would. But for Ethan "there was no way out—none. He was a prisoner for life" (p. 146). The prison, Wharton makes clear by setting the story at the simplest and therefore the most obvious level of society, was the American economic system itself, which laid on most men too much work and responsibility and on most women barely enough variety and adult human contact to keep one's

[handwritten margin note: when the women have / a role to play they are / alive, dead when / + sickly or / they don't have / anything in / life to live for.]

spirit alive. (Significantly, Zeena recovers a degree of cheer and vigor when she has Mattie to take care of.) For every well-trained New Woman like Wharton's Justine Brent, there were thousands of wasted women shut away from corporate life and bitter about their static existences. At least Ethan meets fellow workers when he carts his timber to sale or goes into town for supplies and mail. Farmers' womenfolk normally went nowhere and did nothing but repeat identical tasks in unvaried monotony. To make that isolation of women stark and to emphasize the sterility of life at the level of *Ethan Frome*, Wharton gives the couple no children; and the woman's name she chooses for bold-faced inscription on the only tombstone described in the Frome family plot is also instructive: ENDURANCE (p. 86). If Ethan's life is hard, and it is, woman's is harder yet; and it is sad but not surprising that isolated, housebound women make man feel the full burden of their misery. He is their only connection with the outer world, the vast economic and social system that consigns them to solitary, monotonous domestic lives from which their only escape is madness or death.

[handwritten margin note: Zeena's / misery makes Ethan / feel it.]

In Wharton's fairy tale good girls do not grow up into happy wives, and good-hearted, worthy lovers do not ride off into the western sun with the maiden of their dreams. Most important, witches do not get vanquished and disappear. They multiply. First there is Ethan's mother, then Zeena, then Mattie; and they represent only three of the many women gone "queer" in this wintry American landscape. Wharton's moral is as cold and grim as her Starkfield setting. As long as women are kept isolated and dependent, *Ethan Frome* implies, Mattie Silvers will become Zeena Fromes: frigid crippled wrecks of human beings whose pleasure in life derives from depriving others of theirs. Edith Wharton sneered at the New England realism of Sarah Orne Jewett and Mary Wilkins Freeman, claiming that they looked at the problems of the region through "rose-colored spectacles."[12] The charge is

[handwritten margin note: Trend for / the / women / taking each-others / places]

exaggerated, but not pointless if it is *Ethan Frome* that one uses as the measure.

But why have a young man provide the "vision" of Ethan's story? Why not present *Ethan Frome* directly? A brief look at the tale's evolution is useful here. Edith Wharton began writing Ethan's story in 1906 or 1907 as an exercise in French for her language tutor in Paris.[13] The original sketch, which is really just a fragment, has no narrative frame and suggests that Wharton first conceived her story as nothing more than a piece of realism about rural New England. In the draft, Hart, (the Ethan-figure) is torn between love for Mattie, his wife's niece who lives with them, and fear of his carping, sickly wife, Anna. Anna leaves for two days to see a doctor in Worcester, and Hart spends the evening in town to avoid being alone in the farmhouse with Mattie. He does not want to compromise the girl or risk being discovered with her by his jealous wife, who he suspects may be laying a trap for him. When Anna returns from Worcester she announces that her poor health has forced her to engage a new, more robust serving-girl so Mattie must leave. The fragment ends with Hart and Mattie, hopeless, driving through the snow to the depot, the two of them admitting their love and Mattie, tempted to kill herself, forbidding Hart to leave Anna. / The tempted killing forbids Ethan to leave Zeah a

Although elements of the finished story exist in the early draft, the differences are critical. In the French fragment there is no intimate supper in the wife's absence, no red glass pickle dish, no cat, no suggestion that Anna can haunt her husband (her weapon would be to lay a trap), no echo of Snow-White in the description of Mattie (she has blue eyes and golden curls), no network of symbolic numbers. There are seeds of the later atmosphere in the romanticized descriptions of nature and the vignette of Anna standing in the doorway late at night—ashen, gaunt, menacing.[14] But most of the fairy-tale imagery and symbolism appears only in the finished version of *Ethan Frome*, which Wharton presents to us through the eyes of her narrator. He serves as a surprising double for Ethan. Young and well educated, he is the engineer that Ethan hoped to become, until a series of women blighted his world. (To impress the parallel, they also have in common their compassion for animals, their interest in pure science, and fond memories of a trip to Florida each of them has taken.)

Wharton's use of this particular narrator encourages us to believe that his "vision" of *Ethan Frome* is close to what Ethan's might be, were he able to articulate it. Other people—Harmon Gow and Mrs. Hale, for two—could give us the plain facts of the story. Ethan, Zeena, and Mattie lived together; Zeena hired a new girl and Mattie was forced to leave; Ethan and Mattie took the tragic sled-ride on the evening he drove her to the depot; the three of them, much changed, ended up living together again in permanent poverty and misery. What makes of these facts a fairy tale is the sympathetic young outsider's "vision," the way the transient engineer imagines Zeena as a witch, Mattie as a Snow-White, Ethan as a ruined prince—a man whose head must have sat "gallantly" on his strong shoulders before the accident (p. 6), a man who even in affliction has a profile "like the bronze image of a hero" (p. 15).

The narrator exists to unlock the deepest, the pscyhosexual, level of *Ethan Frome*. Empathically, he projects himself into young Ethan's situation and sees in it the realization of a specific male fear: the fear that woman will turn into witch. The fear that mother will turn into witch (love into hate, day into night, life into death) we all, man or woman, have known. It is the fear, in fact, that the fairy tale *Snow-White* recognizes and deals with constructively, as Bruno Bettelheim explains in *The Uses of Enchantment*.[15] The fear, however, that woman—a larger category than mother—will simply quit serving and, instead, become self-centered and even demanding of service (the fear that Mattie will become Zeena) is a specifically male fear. Women do not expect other women, as a class, to serve them. But men, historically, have expected that deference; and when the expectation is violated, when woman ceases to meet man's needs, the mythic transformation that we see in *Ethan Frome* takes place. As Simone de Beauvoir explains: "In place of the myth of the laborious honeybee or the mother hen is substituted the myth of the devouring female insect: the praying mantis, the spider. . . . The same dialectic makes the erotic object into a wielder of black magic, the servant into a traitress, Cinderella into an ogress, and changes all women into enemies."[16] Precisely this inversion occurs in *Ethan Frome*, and because the terror is man's it makes emotional and intellectual sense to have a man, and one temperamentally close to Ethan, visualize it for us.

In part Wharton treats fear of maternal rejection in *Ethan Frome*. First Ethan's mother abandons his needs; then Zeena, his mother's replacement, does the same. But airy Mattie Silver is not a mother figure and her transformation moves the pattern beyond fear of maternal betrayal to fear of female betrayal in general. That fear plus perpetuation of the social system that makes it well-founded—Mattie Silvers *do* turn into Zeena Fromes—are the combined focus of Wharton's horror story. The tale looks at man's romantic dream of feminine solace and transport and, with a hideous twist, allows Ethan's fantasy to materialize. Mattie Silver does become "his"; but with, rather than without, Zeena; and the two witchlike women hold him prisoner for life in the severely limited economy and social landscape that traps all three of them.

How well the narrator understands the psychological and social problem he dramatizes in *Ethan Frome* is uncertain. Being an ordinary sort of fellow, probably he is a better im-

aginer of its existence than analyst of its meaning. Edith
Wharton, however, stands behind him fully in control of the
tale's depth. As indicated in her choice of the Hawthornian
names Ethan and Zenobia—neither of which is used in the
early French draft—this multileveled book belongs in the
continuum of classic American romance.

The name Ethan and Wharton's gloomy Berkshire setting
bring to mind Hawthorne's "Ethan Brand," the tale of a man
as alienated from woman (though for different reasons) as
Wharton's protagonist. The name Zeena—short for Zenobia—similarly calls up *The Blithedale Romance* (1852), a
book that specifically deals with male fear of woman in two
men, the narrator/participant Coverdale, and the authoritarian perverter of the Blithedale commune, Hollingsworth.
Both men (acting out a pattern that anticipates the moral of
Wharton's cynical early parable, "The Valley of Childish
Things") decide to love childlike Priscilla rather than her
mature sister Zenobia. There is no strict equation between
Hawthorne's and Wharton's books.[17] Neither Ethan nor
Wharton's narrator in *Ethan Frome* is a Hollingsworth, and
neither resembles Hawthorne's Coverdale, a pathetic
would-be poet. But Ethan's and his narrator's mythicized
vision of Mattie Silver—an etherealized virgin-princess for
Ethan to husband and protect—does recall Hollingsworth's
(and conventional Coverdale's) decision in favor of Priscilla.
Furthermore, Wharton's grotesque Zenobia Pierce Frome,
who embodies the fate of Mattie, is the perfect antithesis of
Hawthorne's hearty yet doomed feminist. His Zenobia is
beautiful, healthy, sexual; Wharton's Zeena is ugly, sickly,
frigid. She is, in psychological and mythic terms, the male
dream of Mattie (or Priscilla) brought to its sterile conclusion: she is the adorable blonde from "The Valley of Childish
Things" brought to shriveled middle life. *Ethan Frome* self-
consciously places itself in the tradition of American symbolic fiction and envisions the living death—for women, for

men—that the dream of Mattie Silver implies: crippled females, "queer" women of the region.

In her French draft Edith Wharton explicitly states that Mattie "exemplified all the dull anguish of the long line of women who, for two hundred years, had been buffeted by life and who had eaten out their hearts in the constricted and gloomy existence of the American countryside."[18] In the finished version of *Ethan Frome* Wharton is more subtle, but no less clear. Witchlike Zenobia Frome, a terrifying and repulsive figure archetypally, is in social terms not at all mysterious: it is a commonplace of scholarship about the persecution of witches that many of them were ordinary women bent and twisted by the conditions of their lives as women, their isolation and powerlessness. Stated simply, Zeena Frome is the witch that conservative New England will make of unskilled young Mattie; and Wharton's inverted fairy tale about the multiplication of witches in Ethan's life, a story appropriately told by a horrified young man whose job it is to build the future, finally serves as a lesson in sociology. Witches do exist, Wharton's tale says, and the culture creates them.

In her next book Wharton turns the psychological situation one hundred and eighty degrees and looks at how women have assimilated the male fantasy of heroic rescue and transportation, to their enormous disadvantage. For Prince Charming, *The Reef* demonstrates, is a male, not a female, creation; his success precludes rather than bestows freedom for women.

It is interesting that shortly before *The Reef* was published, Charlotte Perkins Gilman complained in *The Man-Made World*, her 1911 volume, that literature offered an extremely limited and distorted picture of adult experience. Gilman comments briefly on contemporary adventure fiction and moves on: "Now for the main branch—the Love Story. Ninety per cent. of fiction is in this line; this is pre-eminently the major interest of life—given in fiction. What is the love-story, as rendered by this art? It is the story of the pre-marital struggle. It is the Adventures of Him in Pursuit of Her—and it stops when he gets her!" Gilman continues, "The 'love' of our stories is man's love of woman. . . . Woman's love for man, as currently treated in fiction is largely a reflex; it is the way he wants her to feel, expects her to feel." She says in disgust: "Love and love and love—from 'first sight' to marriage. There it stops—just the fluttering ribbon of announcement—'and lived happily ever after.' "[19]

Wharton's novel studies the love story—this "lived happily ever after" myth that peeved Gilman so; and *The Reef*, full of splendid fairy-tale scenes and hopes, does not end happily, much less happily ever after. It ends miserably for all concerned. In an age of uplifting adventure and love novels—the worst perhaps being Harold Bell Wright's best-selling synthesis of the two genres in 1911, *The Winning of Barbara Worth* (Barbara is what is won)—*The Reef* is a contrary book. It is a slow-moving psychological novel: an unadventurous, un-love story about love.

Unlike *Ethan Frome* and *The Custom of the Country*, the books that bracket it in this extraordinarily productive period in her career, *The Reef* was not begun at an earlier time and put aside. Wharton wrote the book from the ground up in very short order and under extremely trying circumstances (chiefly, the complete deterioration of her marriage). She started the novel in the spring of 1911, just a matter of months before *Ethan Frome* appeared in the August issue of *Scribner's* magazine, and she finished it in August 1912. Almost immediately upon its completion she resumed work on *The Custom of the Country*, which she had abandoned three years earlier. It is almost as if *Ethan Frome* freed her to create *The Reef*, which freed her to complete *The Custom of the Country*. If so, it is not hard to see how *Ethan Frome* cleared the way for *The Reef*.

Ethan Frome is complex but not subtle. Like the world it images, the mood of the piece is dark and obviously pessimistic. One could almost accuse the book of being heavy-handed: the fairy-tale symbols are bold, the allegory of Mattie becoming Zeena is literally acted out. *The Reef*, in contrast, is done in pastels. It too dramatizes sexual repression and bitter disillusion with love; but, perhaps because Wharton had already worked the themes through in one context and perspective in *Ethan Frome*, the use of fairy-tale imagery and symbolism in *The Reef* does not result in a new fairy tale but in a normal, full-length novel highly shaded by fairy-tale motifs and themes. *The Reef*, in other words, is not an original fairy tale; it is a conventional novel whose meaning in large measure derives from allusions to two well-known, indeed probably the best-known, fairy tales: *Cinderella* and *Sleeping Beauty*.

The novel is a long, realistic narrative about genteel, sophisticated people whom Wharton brings together at a French château of picture-book charm and beauty. In this setting she interlocks the fates of two couples: the publicly affianced Anna Leath and George Darrow, mature people who have known each other for many years, and the secretly pledged Sophy Viner and Owen Leath, young lovers who have just recently met. Both prospective brides—one a "lady" and the other a New Woman—harbor romantic dreams of female salvation through love and marriage. But Anna's plan to marry George Darrow disintegrates when she learns that he and Sophy, the fiancée of her stepson Owen, and therefore her future daughter-in-law, have been lovers: they met by accident in London and spent a week together before each journeyed to Givré, where they are shocked to see each other. There at the château Sophy becomes engaged to Owen Leath, but because he suspects and Anna discovers Sophy's previous relationship with Darrow, Sophy breaks her engagement to Owen. This quadrangle of fiancés and former lovers is involved. But the outcome is simple. No marriage takes place in *The Reef*, and each woman's dream of deliverance by a man ends in disillusionment to expose the fraudulent romantic visions fostered by the limitations imposed on women—in Sophy's case, economic dependence; in Anna's, sexual repression.

Wharton's older heroine, Anna, grew up (like Wharton herself) in old New York, where she was praised as "a model of ladylike repression."[20] We are told that she was a perfect little girl. She dutifully denied the emotions and desires her elders forbade her even feeling, not to mention expressing, and she idealized the passion she subconsciously wanted to experience and understand. Yet long before the novel opens the child began to tire of her sheltered and restricted life. "Love, she told herself, would one day release her from this spell of unreality" (p. 86). She concludes that marriage, which she envisions as "passion in action, romance converted to reality," will be for her "the magic bridge between West Fifty-fifth Street and life" (pp. 86–87). Rhetoric signals theme. Anna dreamed of becoming a "heroine" who would be "transfigured" by the love of "a man" who would "release her" from a "spell" and with whom marriage would provide the "magic bridge" to "life," the "eternal theme" of which would be their love (pp. 86–87). This language comes from fairy tales because the fantasy itself, not of escaping but of passively being freed, being saved, being awakened and reborn into life by the love of a man—the fantasy, in short, of Sleeping Beauty's being awakened by Prince Charming—comes from fairy tales.

Wharton's manuscript explicitly refers to the fairy tale. In the finished book, Anna Leath and George Darrow, betrothed, spend together at the château de Givré a "perfect" afternoon and evening, during which they discover on the estate "a little old deserted house, fantastically carved and chimneyed, which lay in a moat under the shade of ancient trees" (p. 126). That pleasure house, in an earlier version of the passage, is given a name: "the Sleeping Beauty's lodge." Revisions in Wharton's texts often reveal her wish to avoid the symbolically obtrusive, especially in naming people and places; and this example from *The Reef* is no exception. Her deletion of the direct reference to the Sleeping Beauty, as well as her substitution of the names Givré for Blincourt ("blin[d] court" [ship], hence "the reef") and Darrow for Caringdon (in addition to "don[e] caring," too close to "C[h]ar[m]ing Don"?), suggest that Wharton, far from abandoning the Sleeping Beauty motif, wanted to make it more subtle, lest she insult the reader's intelligence or mar the book's delicate weave of fairy-tale associations by including blatant symbols.[21] The published novel, stripped of obvious allusion (like a building that no longer needs scaffolding), depends on subtle patterns of imagery and symbolism to communicate the fairy-tale motif and its thematic implications.

If lovely Anna Leath, one of the most Jamesian of Wharton's characters (even though the moral of her story is not Jamesian), reminds readers, and rightly so, of Madame de Mauves in the story of the same name and Madame de Cintré in *The American*, or Isabel Archer at the end of *The Portrait of a Lady*, the similarity probably has to do with their disposition as ladies, their well-tended reclusion from the world. As Emily Putnam explained a couple of years before *The Reef* in her scholarly work, *The Lady: Studies in Certain Significant Phases in Her History*, the true lady "can renounce the world more easily than she can identify herself with it. A lady may become a nun in the strictest and poorest order without altering her views of life, without the moral convulsion, the destruction of false ideas, the birth of character that would be the preliminary steps toward becoming an efficient stenographer."[22] What Wharton has her inhibited lady, Anna Summers Leath, confront in *The Reef* is just such a destruction of accultured "false ideas," chief among which is her notion that the love of the right man is the answer to all her problems.

Before the novel opens, Anna thought she found her Prince Charming, her liberator and hero. But marriage soon showed her that the change in her last name from Summers to Leath had contrary significance. The summers of her life were chillingly replaced by a lethean existence at his château de Givré: palace of rime, hoarfrost. The French château which "had called up to her youthful fancy a throng of romantic associations, poetic, pictorial, and emotional," the château which was for Anna "a castle of dreams, evoker of fair images and romantic legend" (pp. 82–83), turned into a chamber of horrors where "life, to Mr. Leath, was like a walk through a carefully classified museum . . . [while] to his wife it was like groping about in a huge dark lumber-room where the exploring ray of curiosity lit up now some shape of breathing beauty and now a mummy's grin" (p. 94). Her husband's kiss, instead of awakening her passionate impulses and desires, "dropped on her like a cold smooth pebble" (p. 91). She and her stepson, Owen, "were like two prisoners who talk to each other by tapping on the wall" (p. 254). In effect, Anna found herself living in a gothicized fairy-tale world, complete with wicked mother-in-law and haunting portrait of a dead first wife—the "exiled consort removed farther and farther from the throne" (p. 97). This was definitely the wrong fairy tale. Anna wanted to be awakened into "contact with the actual business of living" (p. 94); she wanted to be freed, not imprisoned. As Wharton tells us, "the history of Anna Leath appeared to its heroine like some grey shadowy tale that she might have read in an old book, one night as she was falling asleep . . ." (p. 95; Wharton's ellipsis).

Into this midnight tale of frustrated desires comes a rescuer in *The Reef*. Fraser Leath failed, but his widow blames the man, not the dream, and therefore looks forward to marriage with her old friend George Darrow. As she anticipates their reunion at the secluded château, the October sunlight gives the estate such luminescence that Anna

seemed to be opening her own eyes upon it after a long interval of blindness.

The court was very still, yet full of latent life: the wheeling and rustling of pigeons about the rectangular yews and across the sunny gravel; the sweep of rooks above the lustrous greyish-purple slates of the roof, and the stir of the tree-tops as they met the breeze which every day, at that [afternoon] hour, came punctually up from the river.

Just such a latent animation glowed in Anna Leath. In every nerve and vein she was conscious of that equipoise of bliss which the fearful human heart scarce dares acknowledge. She was not used to strong or full emotions; but she had always known that she should not be afraid of them. She was not afraid now; but she felt a deep inward stillness. (p. 83)

Anna is ready for Darrow. Gradually awakening out of a lifetime of abnegation—first as a model daughter, then an obedient wife, finally a decorous widow—the woman's sense of impending freedom erupts. She runs across the grounds like a schoolgirl with "the feeling, which sometimes came to her in dreams, of skimming miraculously over short bright waves" (p. 99).

Anna's running feels dreamlike because, exuberantly uninhibited at last, the "old vicious distinction between romance and reality" (p. 94) for the moment disappears: the prospect of Darrow's arrival arouses the sensuous, carefree spirit so long dormant within Wharton's Sleeping Beauty.

Darrow shares Anna's romantic view of himself. Diplomacy, a princely vocation, will soon send him on a mission to South America, a distant and unfamiliar land, and he means to take his bride with him. Even his kiss is perfect. As in a fairy tale, he is masterful, she responsive, "For a long moment they looked at each other without speaking. She saw the dancing spirit in his eyes turn grave and darken to a passionate sternness. He stooped and kissed her, and she sat as if folded in wings" (p. 115). Transported by this kiss into what seems the "silver tangle of an April wood," Anna's "imagination flew back and forth, spinning luminous webs of feelings between herself and the scene about her" (p. 116). "Her feelings were unlike any she had ever known: richer, deeper, more complete. For the first time everything in her, from head to foot, seemed to be feeding the same full current of sensation" (p. 123). Like the Prince in *Sleeping Beauty*, handsome George Darrow awakens Anna with a kiss, and her dream finally becomes real.

Out of all keeping with fairy-tale expectations, Anna's Prince Charming turns out to be a liar, a hypocrite, a coward, and a libertine. The discovery shocks her into admitting that

her life had ended just as she had dreamed it was beginning. . . . The man who had driven away from her house in the autumn dawn was not the man she had loved; he was a stranger with whom she had not a single thought in common. . . . She had believed it would be possible to separate the image of the man she had thought him from that of the man he was. . . . But now she had begun to understand that the two men were really one. The Darrow she worshipped was inseparable from the Darrow she abhorred. (pp. 301–2)

As the image of Darrow as two men emphasizes, the double standard forms "the reef" on which Anna's dream shatters. As Louis Auchincloss points out: "Before opening *The Reef* the reader must be prepared for a moral climate in which extra-marital physical love is considered damning to a woman and only mildly reprehensible to a man." But Auchincloss errs in implying that Edith Wharton approved of that double standard, a "morality [which now] seems absurd and hypocritical."[23] *The Reef* attacks the double standard.

Sheltered Anna Leath is shocked (yet jealous of Sophy too, we should remember) when she learns of Darrow's brief affair with the younger woman. Her real horror, however, springs from the realization that the double standard not only justifies careless sexual encounters for men but, worse, deception of and contempt for women as a group. Darrow "had come to her with an open face and a clear conscience—come to her from this [the affair with Sophy]! If his security was the security of falsehood it was horrible; if it meant that he had forgotten, it was worse" (p. 294). This reasoning makes sense. As Anna sees it, either Darrow respects her so little that he can glibly lie to her, or he respects Sophy so little that he can casually forget her. Whichever it is, he reveals contempt for one (if not both) of the women. Anna realizes "with a chill of fear that she would never again know if he were speaking the truth or not" and "the idea that his tact was a kind of professional expertness filled her with repugnance" (pp. 324–25, 323). "No doubt," she reflects, "men often had to make such explanations: they had the formulas by heart . . . A leaden lassitude descended on her" (p. 294; Wharton's ellipsis).

Anna tries but cannot renounce Darrow. She clings to him desperately—rationalizing his deceit "by persuading herself that only through such concessions could women like herself hope to keep what they could not give up"—that is, a man (p. 322). Yet she loathes her behavior. "She pictured [her daughter] Effie growing up under the influence of the woman she saw herself becoming—and she hid her eyes from the humiliation of the picture" (p. 335). Indeed she has humiliated herself. But why? Surely, Darrow—a liar and an egotist—is not worth the self-abasement. Partly to blame is biology, more accurately the unnatural suppression of Anna's normal biological needs and desires. She has been repressed for so long that her erotic longings for Darrow overwhelm her; she cannot control her awakened impulses and responses even though they produce a feeling of dependency she hates. The intensity and absolute believability of Anna's dilemma Wharton may very well have been able to communicate so effectively because she herself, quite possibly, experienced similar conflicts toward the end of her affair with Morton Fullerton (despite their erotic and intellectual compatibility, Edith Wharton could not have cut a very pretty picture to herself as she helped her lover get out from under his former mistress's blackmail threats).

Still, sexual repression explains only part of Anna's problem, which is the romantic dream itself: the hope for deliverance through love, with marriage following as a matter of course. As precious to Wharton's heroine as it has been to most women trapped in comatose lives, the fairy-tale fantasy of being rescued by a man must, Wharton shows, be outgrown. (Again, the author's personal experience almost surely led her to this theme.) For the fantasy is pernicious. It teaches women to endure lives they despise, and, while purporting to free them from living death, in fact glorifies abnegation. Sleeping Beauty does not awaken to live her own life; she is awakened to serve as the Prince's grateful and loving dependent, as Wharton underscores by describing Anna's ecstasy when her dream of love appears to be coming true: "She felt like a slave, and a goddess, and a girl in her teens . . ." (p. 124; Wharton's ellipsis). This is the apotheosis of Anna's romantic dream—to feel abased, and etherealized, and immature. The image obviously offends any admirable concept of human self-fulfillment because Anna has not been freed or saved by her Prince Charming. She has been enthralled, in both senses of the word.

The structure of the novel charts the crash of her fantasy. In contrast to the gloomy weather and dingy urban settings of book 1, Anna's idyllic world of latent animation at the château in book 2 does seem a fairy-tale world coming to life. However, the harder she clings to her dream in the face of realities it cannot accommodate, the more inhospitable and enclosed the atmosphere becomes. In book 3 she has "the eerie feeling of having been overswept by a shadow which there had been no cloud to cast" (p. 185). The day turns rainy and its two main events are Anna's visit to an injured child and Darrow's secret meeting with Sophy in a decaying summerhouse. In book 4 Anna does not leave Givré where her dream of perfect love is attenuated as she learns the truth about Darrow's character. The dream dissolves altogether in book 5, which like book 1 takes place mainly in Paris. The atmosphere grows stormy and dark, the action consists of frantic journeys and conferences in hotel rooms, and Anna last appears not at the château but in the bedroom of a strange woman in a shabby Parisian hotel.

This last scene is upsetting, even cruel, as critics often remark. But Wharton makes it so for a reason. Although Anna can no longer delude herself about marrying Darrow, she still clings to her hope of being saved by someone other than herself. She decides "it was Sophy Viner only who could save her—Sophy Viner only who could give her back her lost serenity. She would seek the girl out and tell her that she had given Darrow up; and that step once taken there would be no retracing it, and she would perforce have to go forward alone" (p. 361). If successful, the plan will reanimate her dream: Darrow and Sophy's careless affair will be transformed into a beautiful love-match, and Anna will be transfigured into a self-sacrificing heroine. But Wharton does not let Anna find Sophy and therefore be saved by her. Instead she has her find herself among strangers in a tawdry hotel love-nest, and there all illusion about fairy-tale love explodes. In the person of the slovenly Mrs. McTarvie-Birch at the Hôtel Chicago we finally see the embodiment of Anna's earlier image of the woman in love as "a slave, and a goddess, and a girl in her teens": a prostitute who is bought and owned like a slave, enthroned on her bed like a goddess, and distracted by her pet poodle like a girl in her teens. That Anna mistakes this woman and her pimp for husband and wife simply emphasizes how pathetically naive she still is about the whole subject of love, sex, and marriage.

Wharton does not mock Anna in *The Reef*. (The irony of the final scene is sobering, not amusing or contemptuous.) As Hildegarde Hawthorne declared in 1908 in *Women and Other Women* (a book that, incidentally, singles out Wharton, Gertrude Atherton, and Frances Hodgson Burnett as the three most important novelists of the day): "Woman still labours under the curse of our sex, unreality. It is our besetting sin, probably the legitimate heritage of a long train of events, of handicaps, of makeshifts." She continues: "To live within a plaster cast, however graceful its stride or comely its exterior, is neither dignified nor healthful. Better to smash it and stagger out with whatever lack of balance and odd contortions may supervene." This, according to Hawthorne, who is optimistic, "woman has accomplished," though her first steps do appear awkward and "wavering."[24] Surely Wharton would agree on the issue of women trapped in unreality; Anna is a perfect example of the problem. That real progress has been made breaking out of the "plaster cast," however, is another question, and one on which Wharton is pessimistic. She tells Anna's story to confute a fantasy of romantic love much cherished by women and argues that women will never be free so long as they cling to fairy-tale myths that tell them to look to men to "save" them. The target of criticism in *The Reef* is not Anna and not really even women as a class, although the book does attack ideas held by women—held because they are carefully taught to hold them. (No one is born knowing, or believing in, the myth of Sleeping Beauty.) Wharton's object of attack is the culture that represses women and encourages them to believe that love and marriage will someday release them into "reality." Love and marriage as the culture defines them are not a release. Anna's dream cannot even withstand an engagement, let alone marriage, which, as her first union demonstrated and her relationship with Darrow suggests, simply delivers a woman from one subservient life into another.

But Anna, one must admit, hardly represents the typical American woman of the prewar decade. In addition to being rich and Europeanized, she is a hangover from the previous century, the type of woman sociologist Mary Roberts Coolidge discusses in *Why Women Are So*, published the same year as *The Reef*, 1912: the nineteenth-century woman who was repressed in childhood and irrelevantly educated in adolescence. Her enforced ignorance about sexuality, including pregnancy and childbirth, according to Coolidge, often created psychological disorders; and it is no wonder that she was timid about life and her interests often narrowed to a trivial feminine "sphere." Coolidge's analysis of the problem concludes with a vision of the future, already coming to pass in her opinion, when both sexes will abandon the anachronism of "superfeminine" and "supermasculine" ideals. All human beings will move toward the center, men becoming more domestic and active as fathers, women becoming more intellectual and active in the world.

Wharton's characterization of Anna Leath's foil, Sophy Viner, almost seems designed for the express purpose of deflating the optimism of theorists like Mary Roberts Coolidge. Sophy is a twentieth-century woman, a New Woman: she is modern, self-confident, practical. She is also completely unable to free herself from certain traditional notions and impediments. Her lack of marketable skills, her vulnerability to the double standard, and her own romantic infatuation with George Darrow keep her from gaining authority over her own life. She ends where she began, the unhappy appendage to a loud American dowager on the loose in Europe.

Sophy has neither the class nor the culture of an Anna Leath; she is far more ordinary. (It is hard to imagine Anna's having gone to school with someone named "Mamie Hoke," for example.) Sophy in addition is more experienced. An orphan since childhood, she is at twenty-four "distinguished from the daughters of wealth by her avowed acquaintance with the real business of living, a familiarity as different as possible from their theoretical proficiency" (p. 26). As a consequence, she is emphatically up-to-date. "Oh, I never mean to marry," she announces early in the novel. "I'm not so sure that I believe in marriage. You see I'm all for self-development and the chance to live one's life. I'm awfully modern, you know" (p. 61). Sophy's glib rhetoric somewhat undercuts her declaration. But in light of her native candor and the marriages she has seen (plus the proposals she has had from repulsive widowers), her wish never to marry and her skepticism about the institution in general should be taken as seriously as Lily Bart's fear of marriage in *The House of Mirth*.

Sophy wants to be an actress. Financial need has always kept her from trying her luck, but when *The Reef* opens she has a sensible plan; she hopes to earn enough money as a governess in Paris to pay for acting lessons. The plan does not work out. She can find no position in Paris and poverty forces her to accept the job of governess at Givré, hours away from the city. Her decision to marry Anna Leath's stepson, Owen, and stay at the château is just the next logical consequence of her economic predicament (she does not want to remain a governess the rest of her life) and of the compromises she is forced to make despite her aspirations as an "awfully modern" young woman.

Sophy faces the dilemma of Lily Bart and all women who were not independently wealthy: freedom for anyone requires economic security; economic security for women required marriage; marriage required loss of freedom for women. Sophy capitulates to the inevitable. As her later admission that she does not love Owen Leath confirms, she decides to marry for money. In the end, to her credit, she changes her mind and bravely decides not to contract herself to a man she does not love. (Perhaps the name Owen—owe/own—was chosen to suggest the kind of husband he would make.) The alternative of resuming her parasitic life as some socialite's baggage is detestable. But no other choice presents itself, which is Wharton's point: this talented, ambitious young woman has no way of wresting control over her own life. The notion sometimes advanced by critics that Wharton is cruel to Sophy because she makes her sister, Mrs. McTarvie-Birch, a prostitute and has Anna (and bear in mind it is not Wharton, but Anna) see a resemblance between the two sisters at the end of *The Reef* is as misguided as accusing Wharton of cruelty toward Mattie Silver or Lily Bart. The fact is, the novel's last scene implicitly admires rather than punishes Sophy Viner: against all odds, she has managed so far to avoid her sister's fate.

In addition to its realistic social criticism, Sophy's plot completes Wharton's commentary on fairy tales in *The Reef*. Literally Sophy serves as a foil for Anna; she is the New Woman whose experience with life highlights the older woman's naiveté. But as with Zeena and Mattie, symbolically more important than the contrasts between the two women are the similarities and connections. Both love the same man, Darrow. Both are closely attached to another man, Owen—Sophy as his fiancée, Anna as his stepmother (making her, in an echo of the sexual rivalry in *Ethan Frome*, a potential stepmother figure for Sophy). But, because Anna and Owen "have always been on odd kind of brother-and-sister terms" (p. 114), Anna usually thinks of herself as Owen's sister, which makes Sophy more like Anna's future sister than daughter-in-law. Indeed, if Sophy were to marry Owen, Anna and Sophy, like sisters, would share the same mother-figure (Madame de Chantelle) just as they now share the care of the same child (Effie). The intertwining of the two women's identities to imply figurative sisterhood suggests that symbolically Anna Leath and Sophy Viner represent a split heroine, a dichotomous embodiment of one basic identity. That basic identity in *The Reef* is the would-be fairy-tale heroine who is rescued from a miserable life by some sort of Prince Charming hero. For if Anna Leath resembles Sleeping Beauty, waiting for a man's passion to animate her, Sophy Viner in her way recalls the tale of Cinderella—a poor, neglected, down-to-earth girl who is transported to riches by her Prince Charming.

Especially reminiscent of Cinderella in book 1, Sophy Viner appears remarkably cheerful in the face of hardship; and for a woman in her middle twenties, she has an uncommonly fresh, juvenile quality. Her physical appearance and movements often look "boyish" to Darrow, so spontaneous and guileless she seems, while her earthy "naturalness" is so pronounced that she, like Mattie Silver before her, reminds the man who desires her of "a dryad in a dew-drenched forest" (p. 34; note also her surname).[25] Like Cinderella setting out for the ball, Sophy emerges dressed for the theater "looking as if she had been plunged into some sparkling element which had curled up all her drooping tendrils and wrapped her in a shimmer of fresh leaves" (p. 34). Her exuberance transfigures her and tricks Darrow into believing her old outfit "some miracle" of French dressmaking (p. 34). In fact, her whole adventure in Paris—sightseeing, dining out, attending the theater—seems a fairy tale come true; and George Darrow obviously plays the hero. "Do you want to know what I feel?" she asks him and then exclaims: "That you're giving me the only chance I've ever had!" Very like Cinderella at the moment of transformation from peasant to princess, Sophy marvels: "Is it true? Is it really true? Is it really going to happen to *me*?" (p. 71). The answer is both yes and no.

Sophy Viner gets her adventure, enjoys it, and never regrets it. But this miraculous adventure does not conclude in her living happily ever after with her Prince Charming, nor with his surrogate, Owen Leath, at his gorgeous château; and the moral of Sophy's plot mirrors that of Anna's. Whether the

Cinderella myth of economic salvation or the Sleeping Beauty myth of sensual/spiritual salvation, the fairy-tale fantasy of being saved by a man from a life of misery is an illusion that ends in disillusion.

Precisely that happens in *The Reef*. Each woman's dream comes true and, in doing so, results in disillusionment. Both women are rescued by a man only to discover that the rescue brings with it unsuspected disadvantages. George Darrow does awaken Anna Leath's repressed sexuality, and she therefore feels sensuously and emotionally aware for the first time in her life. Owen Leath does promise to marry Sophy Viner, and she can therefore anticipate economic security and luxury for the first time in her life. The terrible irony is that, while each rescue is successful, it is at the same time self-defeating. Anna discovers that sexual expression does not entitle her to express herself fully but requires the suppression of many other emotions and desires. Her fantasy comes true, but she is still only a partial being. Similarly, Sophy discovers that luxury and economic security will not entitle her to the freedom she really wants and that life with Owen Leath will not be pleasurable. Her dream promises to come true, but she will still be a dependent and perforce compliant person. Wharton's thematic logic is subtle yet unmistakable. Even as rescue by a man fulfills the letter of the fairy-tale fantasy, it is false to its supposed spirit. For if a woman looks to a man as her deliverer, she acquiesces in the dispensation of superior power to men and consequently must accept as just and moral the subordination of women, which condones the double standard and the idea of male proprietorship.

The weakness in *The Reef* is Wharton's characterization of the men. Whereas Ethan Frome is presented as a sympathetic character, one who is very much the victim of his circumstances, Wharton makes George Darrow so self-centered and Owen Leath so weak that one could accuse her of stacking the deck and therefore miss, or dismiss, her criticism of institutionalized fantasies; she comes close in *The Reef*, as she did on a number of occasions from *Bunner Sisters* on, to attacking men per se rather than ideas they are taught to have about women and their relation to them. Perhaps Wharton, whose dislike for Darrow and Owen is obvious, takes out on them the contempt she may have felt for all lovers and husbands in the years immediately following her affair with Fullerton and just preceding her final break with Teddy. In any case her treatment of the two men is exceptionally harsh, even for her. Still, her argument is sound and deserves attention.

In the myth Prince Charming frees or brings to new life his heroine—Sleeping Beauty or Cinderella (notice that she, but not he, changes names and identities)—so that she may become his human re-creation and possession. Likewise in *The Reef* George Darrow has toward women "the male instinct of ownership" (p. 17). Before he becomes her lover, Sophy reminds him of "a terra-cotta statuette, some young image of grace hardly more than sketched in the clay" (p. 71); and he regrets not having been able to bring Anna to life when she was younger. He thinks: "If she had been given to him then he would have put warmth in her veins and light in her eyes: would have made her a woman through and through. . . . A love like his might have given her the divine gift of self-renewal" (p. 29). Magnanimous as it sounds, this Pygmalion attitude reflects astounding masculine egoism. As Wharton explains, sarcastically:

The women he had frequented had either been pronouncedly "ladies" or they had not. Grateful to both for ministering to the more complex masculine nature, and disposed to assume that they had been evolved, if not designed, to that end, he had instinctively kept the two groups apart in his mind. . . . He liked, above all, people who went as far as they could in their own line—liked his "ladies" and their rivals to be equally unashamed of showing for exactly what they were. (p. 25)

Thus, Sophy Viner, not a "lady" in his opinion, exists for George Darrow's diversion, for his sexual gratification.

Anna Leath, in contrast, he prizes like a fine object of art or a spirited horse he plans to own. Looking forward to "the high privilege of possessing her," he displays little erotic interest in Anna, a "lady," but exults: "Pride and passion were in the conflict—magnificent qualities in a wife! . . . Yes! It was worth a great deal to watch that fight between her instinct and her intelligence, and know one's self the object of the struggle" (pp. 128, 129, 130–31). She reminds him of "a picture so hung that it can be seen only at a certain angle: an angle known to no one but its possessor. The thought flattered his sense of possessorship . . . " (p. 129; Wharton's ellipsis).

In the character of George Darrow, Wharton reveals the real values implicit in the Prince Charming fantasy. The self-acknowledged savior of women, Darrow believes they exist solely for his pleasure, and he has no difficulty fitting Sophy Viner and Anna Leath into his two categories of women: sexual objects or decorative objects but in neither case autonomous people. Women, in effect, represent human property at his disposal. The love of this man, or any man sharing his "traditional views," cannot possibly rescue any woman from a life of involuntary self-denial.

Simone de Beauvoir remarks on the male orientation of the Sleeping Beauty and Cinderella myths (which she too considers together): "What would Prince Charming have for occupation if he had not to awaken the Sleeping Beauty? . . . The Cinderella myth . . . flourishes especially in prosperous countries like America. How should the men there spend their surplus money if not upon a woman?" Beauvoir continues: "It is clear that in dreaming of himself as donor, liberator, redeemer, man still desires the subjection of woman; for in order to awaken the Sleeping Beauty, she must have been put to sleep; ogres and dragons must be about if there are to be captive princesses. . . . What he requires in his heart of hearts is that this struggle remain a game for him, while for woman it involves her very destiny. Man's true victory, whether he is liberator or conqueror, lies just in this: that woman freely recognizes him as her destiny."[26] It is against this concept of female destiny that Edith Wharton argues in *The Reef*. The fairy-tale fantasy of deliverance by a man appears to be but is not a dream of freedom for women. It is a glorification of the status quo: a culturally perpetuated myth of female liberation which in reality celebrates masculine dominance, proprietorship, and privilege. That reality, for both of Edith Wharton's heroines, in the end marks "the reef." As Beauvoir would put it almost half a century later: "A myth always implies a subject who projects his hopes and his fears toward a sky of transcendence. Women do not set themselves up as Subject and hence have erected no virile myth in which their projects are reflected; they have no religion or poetry of their own; they still dream through the dreams of men."[27]

Prince Charming, properly understood, "liberates" his heroine into a life of permanent dependence. Exactly that happens in morbid *Ethan Frome*, just as it threatens to happen in *The Reef*; and love based on a model of slavery, even if that model comes from splendid fairy tales, can in Wharton's opinion free no one, man or woman. That said, she was through with the subject for a while and back—with a vengeance—to the hard, loveless issues of marriage and money, but with a twist. *The Custom of the Country*, like her life, admits divorce.

The Business of Marriage

Emily Putnam observed in 1910, three years before *The Custom of the Country* was published: "In defiance of the axiom that he who works, eats, the lady who works has less to eat than the lady who does not. There is no profession open to her that is nearly as lucrative as marriage, and the more lucrative the marriage the less work it involves."[1] By the time *The Custom of the Country* appeared in 1913, Putnam's principle, given theorists such as Gilman and Veblen before her, was a commonplace of feminist criticism; Wharton herself had given the idea qualified dramatic rendering as early as 1905 in *The House of Mirth* with its contrast between the marriages, for example, of Judy Trenor and Nettie Struther. No doubt, Wharton would, as I have suggested, have argued with Putnam that the lady who is married *does* have work to do; the work, as Veblen explains, of conspicuously consuming for her wealthy husband as living testimony to his pecuniary prowess. But at the same time Wharton would not have disagreed with the characterization of marriage as a profession, and the most lucrative one available, for a woman seeking status and power in American society. Her brash, ambitious heroine Undine Spragg successfully plots her whole life on that principle in *The Custom of the Country*.

The novel is Wharton's tour de force on the marriage question (and perhaps, the best novel she ever wrote): it throws a brilliant, satiric light on the institution of marriage, stripping it of all sentiment and sentimentality. The key is Undine herself. Unlike Lily Bart, she does not fear marriage as a threat to her autonomy. Unlike Justine Brent or Anna Leath, she has no illusions about the marriage union as a bond of love which will perfect her personal happiness or complete her personality. And she would never, like poor romantic Mattie Silver, choose death over separation from a man she wants to marry. Instead, like Sophy Viner but entirely without her scruples, Undine approaches marriage as a simple economic contract in which both parties have well-defined, mutually aggrandizing, agreed-upon roles; and because she accepts the commercial nature of matrimony and is willing to negotiate herself on the marriage market (which she manages to do not just once, but four times), Undine is unique among Wharton's early heroines. She controls her own life. First she marries a loyal son of old New York, Ralph Marvell; then she marries an elegant French nobleman, the Marquis Raymond de Chelles; then she remarries her first husband, Elmer Moffatt, who always showed spunk but who now, as a newly rich multimillionaire capitalist, also shows a fabulous cheque book.

Wharton's own feelings about her heroine clearly were intense yet divided. As both R. W. B. Lewis and Cynthia Griffin Wolff point out, and they are surely correct, Wharton cast Undine as her opposite—ignorant, intrepid, unintrospective—yet also as her twin: Undine's energy, her anger and pride, her love of travel and gorgeous clothing and her impatience with failure and shabbiness—these, although exaggerated and simplified in the fictional character, do bring to mind the author herself.

The buried affinity probably explains why Edith Wharton had a difficult time writing *The Custom of the Country*. She started it in 1908 after completing *The Fruit of the Tree*, which was published in 1907. But she put it aside, not coming back to her devastating heroine until after she had finished *Ethan Frome* and *The Reef*. Originally *Scribner's* had wanted to begin serializing the novel in January 1909; but the love affair with Morton Fullerton followed by the last ugly stages of her breakup with Teddy, fights and bitter misunderstandings that climaxed in her decision in 1911 to sell her Massachusetts home, "The Mount," kept her from successfully resuming work on the novel. Then her long stagnation on the book broke, not surprisingly, at about the same time that her marriage collapsed completely. She signed the final sale papers on "The Mount" in June 1912, finished *The Reef* in August, picked the story about Undine back up in the autumn and had enough done for serialization to begin in January 1913. On April 16, 1913 her divorce from Teddy was formally decreed by a Parisian court; by August she had completed the novel.

If there is an undeniable ferocity about the book it is probably because *The Custom of the Country* was freed—let loose—from Edith Wharton's imagination by her final break with her own husband. In biographical terms, if *Ethan Frome* and *The Reef* served to help get the romance with Fullerton out of her system, *The Custom of the Country* seems to have done the same for her unfortunate marriage. After years of smothered resentments and then terrible quarrels, which settled on money as the issue to wound each other with (rather than focus on their far deeper problems of sexual and intellectual incompatibility), Edith Wharton must have felt enormous relief to be able to pile divorce upon divorce in *The Custom of the Country*. It makes sense that, until her own freedom from marriage was secured and official, she would be unable to complete Undine's story: personally, divorce was repugnant to Wharton; but so was marriage in many respects, and *The Custom of the Country* gave her the opportunity to attack both with vehemence.

The novel also allowed her to enter Undine, a compelling but in some ways vicious character, in the lists of American heroines, which by 1913 overbrimmed with attractive, blithe New Women whose authors led them through remarkable adventures that typically stopped at the altar. In terms of plot, Wharton drew most obviously on a story written by her friend Robert Grant, *Unleavened Bread* (1900), a best-seller that was unusual, though hardly unique, in *not* holding the New Woman up for admiration and *not* stopping with marriage. Grant's heroine, Selma Babcock, then Selma Babcock Littleton, then Selma Babcock Littleton Lyons, uses marriage, much as Undine does, as her means of moving up the social ladder. Along the way to becoming the wife of a United States senator she discards two husbands who fail to keep up with her notions of status and social prominence. Divorce has no more sting or stigma for Selma than it does for Undine, or Undine's girlhood friend Indiana Frusk, whose career even more closely follows Selma's in scaling, by means of divorce, to the heights of being a famous senator's wife.

Wharton enjoyed Grant's book and was definitely influenced by it: her heroine and his both come from small towns, are ambitious, have no qualms about divorce, and remain supremely confident throughout of their moral rectitude. Nevertheless there is a major difference in the authors' attitudes toward their subject matter. Grant has absolutely no sympathy for Selma, or interest in her beyond capturing her as a "type," the laughable modern clubwoman who bounds from cause to cause (and in this case husband to husband as well) in restless quest of something entertaining yet also morally righteous to do with her otherwise pointless life. In *The Custom of the Country* it is almost as if Wharton, inspired by Grant's book, went on to answer his shallow portrait of the female opportunist with her own tough economic analysis of the basic issue involved, which she, unlike Grant, knows is quite serious: marriage as woman's business in life. As Charlotte Perkins Gilman phrased the truism in *Women and Economics* at the turn of the century: "To the young woman confronting life there is the same world beyond [as there is to the young man], there are the same human energies and human desires and ambitions within. But all that she may wish to have, all that she may wish to do, must come through a single channel and a single choice. Wealth, power, social distinction, fame—not only these, but home and happiness, reputation, ease and pleasure, her bread and butter—all, must come to her through a small gold ring."[2] We may not admire Undine's avaricious approach to marriage, but neither can we fault it as illogical or perverse; it is simply realistic.

Indeed, Undine has seemed so real that Edmund Wilson has called her, in rather ugly language, "the prototype in fiction of the 'gold-digger,' of the international cocktail bitch" and many critics have followed his lead by arguing that the novel is flawed by Wharton's animosity toward her heroine, an uncouth bounder whose greed and ignorance she finds repellent.[3] It is true that Undine Spragg has little to recommend her. She forgets her five-year-old son's birthday. She has the Marvell heirloom jewels reset. She ignores a cable about her husband's illness while she vacations in Europe and then, while he is close to death, takes up with another man. She proposes that her next husband sell the family château in order to have ready cash to lavish on her. Undine shares her water sprite namesake's ability to attract men—Millard Binch, Elmer Moffatt, Aaronson, Popple, Ralph Marvell, Peter Van Degen, Raymond de Chelles—and also appears sirenlike in her heartless exploitation of them. After all, it is "the feeling of power that came with the sense of being loved"[4] that appeals to her. This heroine, in short, does seem a modern Circe: cruel, destructive, misandrous; and *The Custom of the Country* can be read as a conservative satire on the nouveaux-riches invaders who threatened the leisure-class values Edith Wharton grew up with.

Such a view, however, mistakes the superficial for the real object of attack in the novel. Not Undine Spragg, self-centered and insensitive as she is, but the institution of marriage in the leisure class is the main target of Wharton's satire in *The Custom of the Country*. The point about Undine is that, as something of an outsider and therefore a "naïf," she does not bother with the hypocritical rhetoric that rationalizes marriage—she sees what marriage is rather than what people say it is and she acts on what she sees. Consequently, her behavior and her assimilated values reflect Wharton's criticism less of the parvenu than of the established American upper class, which in her view, as in Veblen's, is looked to as the ideal by all of American culture and thus epitomizes pervasive American attitudes (even if not practices) toward women. That is, Edith Wharton *uses* Undine to reveal her criticism of the attitudes implicit in leisure-class marriage, an institution that has long, and unfortunately, been the envy of women dreaming of freedom but that in fact encourages the husband to assert his autonomy as an international playboy like Peter Van Degen or as a manager in the business world (a financier on Wall Street or a lawyer in a prestigious legal firm) while the wife, expected to be supportive and dependent, must channel her desires for self-assertion into the role of conspicuous consumer for him. Her life, in contrast to her husband's, is by definition parasitic and vicarious.

Although the solution offered by Charles Bowen, a wise older man in *The Custom of the Country*, is paternalistic, his analysis of the problem is sound. Taking "a general view of the whole problem of American marriages," he concludes that the weak point is "the fact that the average American looks down on his wife" (p. 205). He charges: "Where does the real life of most American men lie? In some woman's drawing-room or in their offices? The answer's obvious, isn't it? The emotional centre of gravity's not the same in the two hemispheres [Europe and America]. In the effete societies it's love, in our new one it's business. In America the real *crime passionnel* is a 'big steal'—there's more excitement in wrecking railways than homes" (p. 207). "And what's the result—how do the women avenge themselves?" Bowen asks and then remarks: "All my sympathy's with them, poor deluded dears, when I see their fallacious little attempts to trick out the leavings tossed them by the preoccupied male—the money and the motors and the clothes—and pretend to themselves and each other that *that's* what really constitutes life!" (p. 208). Bowen goes on to identify the main point of *The Custom of the Country* when he dubs Undine "a monstrously perfect result of the system: the completest proof of its triumph" (p. 208). For Wharton dramatizes her criticism of marriage ironically in this novel. She focuses on the marriage market not as it victimizes one of Bowen's "poor deluded dears" but as it is successfully played by one fiercely ambitious and highly imitative young woman. Ever since she was a little girl out in the midwest, where she used to " 'play lady' before the wardrobe mirror" (p. 22), Undine Spragg has longed for status among the fashionably rich. *The Custom of the Country* simply shows how she goes through three marriages, two divorces, one annulment, several engagements, and one lover to achieve that goal.

When the novel opens, the Spraggs have been installed in New York for two years hoping that Undine, on the strength of her good looks and her father's money, will be admitted to the ranks of the socially elite. Though that hope has not yet been fulfilled, the whole family perseveres. Mr. Spragg continues to accumulate wealth to keep his daughter well-furbished and properly displayed. Mrs. Spragg stoically endures impersonal hotel-life and fancies she contributes to the cause because her masseuse, Mrs. Heeny, enters the portals of New York's rich and famous as familiarly as Mrs. Spragg might have stepped next door back home in Apex. Undine keeps herself beautiful, studies "Boudoir Chat" in the newspaper, and vows "to trust less to her impulses—especially in the matter of giving away rings" to imposters like the supposedly aristocratic Aaronson, an Austrian riding-master she met in Central Park (p. 26). Her social career begins, in other words, as a group enterprise, a family investment in the leisure class. Although her parents do not aspire to membership themselves, they agree that her social ambitions are worthy and sensible. For Undine is no libertine. She may appear "*diverse et ondoyante*" (p. 83), but her underlying values and motives are as uncomplicated as her small-town background. "She wanted, passionately and persistently, two things which she believed should subsist together in any well-ordered life: amusement and respectability; and despite her surface-sophistication her notion of amusement was hardly less innocent than when she hung on the plumber's fence with Indiana Frusk" in Apex (p. 354).

Even conservative, upper-class Ralph Marvell, though he disapproves of his wife's desires when he finally understands them, recognizes their innocence. Midway through the novel he realizes "it was admiration, not love, that she wanted. She wanted to enjoy herself, and her conception of enjoyment was publicity, promiscuity—the band, the banners, the crowd, the close contact of covetous impulses, and the sense of walking among them in cool security" (pp. 223–24). Ralph is correct. Undine invades the leisure class primarily to show herself off: she just wants the best possible mirror to reflect her belief that she is extraordinary.

In a deeper sense, though, Undine desires the publicity she associates with status in the leisure class because "public triumph . . . was necessary to her personal enjoyment" (p. 549). The important word is triumph. Undine is fiercely competitive and determined to win. Of the Fairfords and Marvells, old New York families, she says to Mrs. Heeny: "I want the best. Are they as swell as the Driscolls and Van Degens?" Assured they are even better, she exalts (again in front of the mirror): "There were to be no more mistakes and no more follies now! She was going to know the right people at last—she was going to get what she wanted!" (pp. 24, 29). Undine wants power—the kind of power over people and circumstances which will enable her to be a social "triumph," one of the leisure-class potentates who personify her concept of success.

Nowhere is this love of power more significantly expressed than in the image Wharton associates with Undine when she appears at the opera, engaged to marry a brahmin. "Now at last she was having what she wanted—she was in conscious possession of the 'real thing'; and through her other, more diffused, sensations Ralph's adoration gave her such a last refinement of pleasure as might have come to some warrior Queen borne in triumph by captive princes, and reading in the eyes of one the passion he dared not speak" (pp. 98–99). The image of a warrior queen borne in triumph by captive princes not only describes the structure of *The Custom of the Country*, which Wharton called a "chronicle-novel"[5] and which, in place of a conventional plot, recounts a series of campaigns, each followed by its brief "progress" in the regal sense of the term. The image also describes Undine's character: her capacity to wield and embody power. By nature aggressive, assertive, confident, and ambitious, Undine is at the same time manipulative, theatrical, and adaptable. Reared as the family princess, she has all the requisites of a warrior queen, and the book chronicles the fierce social campaigns she wages in order to capture the right princes.

There is a primitivism about Wharton's image, and Undine's character in general, that roots this novel not only in Veblenesque socioeconomics but also in feminist anthropological assumptions popular at the turn of the century. Hildegarde Hawthorne in 1908 exclaimed in disgust: "Whence that absurd term 'New Woman'?" Strong women were not new in her opinion,[6] any more than they were, for example, in Anna Garlin Spencer's or Charlotte Perkins Gilman's or Olive Schreiner's. All of these theorists, and they are

typical, argue that the contemporary woman's female ances-
tor was man's complete equal—if not his superior—with respect to vigor, economic production, and inventiveness.
Spencer, for instance, begins her study *Woman's Share in
Social Culture* (1912) with a chapter on "The Primitive
Working-Woman" (it is the groundwork for her next chapter,
"The Ancient and Modern Lady"), and her anthropological
claims for woman as the race's first inventor and manufac-
turer were by no means new in 1912. Many years earlier it
was decided that woman was in fact the race's original industrial genius. Indeed, part of the purpose of the Woman's Building in 1893 (and it had to be a conservative venture, of
course, to be included in the Chicago Exposition) was to
impress that idea upon the public. As the all-female Board of
Managers announced in 1892: "It will be shown that women,
among all the primitive peoples, were the originators of most
of the industrial arts, and that it was not until these became
lucrative that they were appropriated by men, and women
pushed aside. . . . Woman constructed the rude semblance
of a home. She dressed and cooked the game. . . . She cured
and dressed the skins. . . . She invented the needle. . . . She
invented the shuttle. . . . She was the first potter. . . . She
originated basket-making. . . . She learned to ornament
these articles."[7]

This pride in woman's ancestry permeates Olive
Schreiner's *Woman and Labour*, a best-seller in America in
1912 (one year before *The Custom of the Country* was completed). Schreiner takes the argument out of the home and
gives it military dimension:

> The truth is, we are not new. . . .
> We have in us the blood of a womanhood that was never bought
> and never sold; that wore no veil, and had no foot bound. . . . We are
> women of a breed whose racial ideal was no Helen of Troy, passed
> passively from male hand to male hand, as men pass gold or lead;

but that of Brynhild whom Segurd found, clad in helm and byrne, the warrior maid. . . .
We are of a race of women that of old knew no fear, and feared no death. . . . If you would understand us, go back two thousand years, and study our descent. . . . We are the daughters of our fathers as well as of our mothers.[8]

Undine Spragg, fresh out of the raw midwestern regions of America that both alarmed and fascinated Edith Wharton for their sheer vigor and crudity, is Wharton's first contribution to popular anthropology (next would be Charity Royall in *Summer* and then the tribal sexual politics of *The Age of Innocence*); and Wharton's thoughts on the subject, although they are expressed with great sophistication, concur with contemporary notions. She makes Undine, who we are told can stare down her opponent (even her father) like an "Amazon" (p. 124), both a warrior and an entrepreneur.

Kingdoms, in Wharton's twentieth-century America, are won on the stock exchange. Wall Street is the field of battle for the modern robber baron, and although his female counterpart, the modern "warrior Queen," is denied that battleground, she is given her own stock exchange: the institution of marriage in which she herself is the stock exchanged. To create her empire, she invests herself in the right marriage—an enterprise Undine understands and embraces. In fact, she is so highly motivated by a "business shrewdness which was never quite dormant in her" (p. 354) and so confident of her objective, that her ambitiousness puzzles Ralph Marvell. "He wondered from what source Undine's voracious ambitions had been drawn: all she cared for, and attached importance to, was as remote from her parents' conception of life as her impatient greed from their passive stoicism" (pp. 317–18). Ralph cannot see the familial connection because he sees Mr. Spragg in the drawing room, rather than the counting room. As Wharton explains the student of inheritance might have wondered whence Undine derived her overflowing activity. The answer would have been obtained by observing her father's business life. From the moment he set foot in Wall Street Mr. Spragg became another man. Physically the change revealed itself only by the subtlest signs. As he steered his way to his office through the jostling crowd of William Street his relaxed muscles did not grow more taut or his lounging gait less desultory. . . . It was only in his face that the difference was perceptible . . . showing itself now and then in the cautious glint of half-closed eyes, the forward thrust of black brows, or a tightening of the lax lines of the mouth. (p. 119)

Undine is her father's daughter. They have the same "scowl" (p. 59), the same kind of "resolute will" (p. 43), and the same business cunning and enthusiasm. When "resolutely bent on a definite object," Undine is "too sternly animated by her father's business instinct to turn aside in quest of casual distractions" (p. 236). Wharton compares her manipulation of Peter Van Degen with her father's financial maneuvering— "So Mr. Spragg might have felt at the tensest hour of the Pure Water move" (p. 294)—while her decision to live with Peter Van Degen is "as carefully calculated as the happiest Wall Street 'stroke' " (p. 364). Ralph Marvell's wry speculation that modern leisure-class marriages ought to be "transacted on the Stock Exchange" (p. 78) is an idea Undine would no doubt consider very sensible. Wharton's "warrior Queen" has a passion for the business of negotiating herself on the marriage market.

Unlike Lily Bart in *The House of Mirth*, this heroine does not fear marriage as a threat to her independence. To Popple's jocular "I can paint you! He [Ralph] can't forbid that, can he? Not before marriage, anyhow!' " Undine responds with "joyous defiance": "I guess he isn't going to treat me any different afterward" (p. 100). And if she does not believe that the proprietorship of marriage will affect her, neither does Undine share with Justine Brent in *The Fruit of the Tree* a vision of husband and wife as partners mutually engaged in meaningful social work. The only social work that interests Undine Spragg is the leisure-class wife's business of publicly displaying her husband's wealth, and therefore power, by consuming for him in ostentatious splendor.

In fact, *The Custom of the Country* is one of America's great business novels. It belongs in the tradition of Howells's *The Rise of Silas Lapham* (1885), *A Hazard of New Fortunes* (1890), and *The Landlord at Lion's Head* (1897), from the first two of which (if not from all three) Edith Wharton borrowed for her novel. The way Silas Lapham carries himself in his office, propping his feet up on his scrap basket while he talks with Bartley Hubbard in the opening scene of Howells's book, echoes in Wharton's description of Abner Spragg at the end of book 1 in *The Custom of the Country* when Elmer Moffatt talks money with him at his office. Likewise, the literary device of the disastrous formal dinner at which the nouveaux riches horrify their genteel old-money-hosts, Wharton surely took from Howells. Silas's drunken bragging at the Coreys' quiet dinner for him produces the same effect on his hosts as Undine's offhand chatter about divorce—"He isn't in the right set, and I think Mabel realizes she'll never really get anywhere till she gets rid of him" (p. 94)—does on her blueblooded hosts, the Marvells, at their elegant small engagement dinner for her. Probably Wharton even took the name for her successful capitalist in *The Custom of the Country*, Elmer Moffatt, from Howells's Moffitt, Indiana, the birthplace of his aging capitalist, Dryfoos, in *A Hazard of New Fortunes*. In any event, her novel, like Howells's, and then some of Norris's and Dreiser's, takes the ambitious capitalist for its subject and arrives, by means of that focus, at a critique of large areas of American life.

That the capitalist of most importance in *The Custom of the Country* is a woman is unusual, but not without precedent. Three years earlier, in *The Iron Woman* (a best-seller in 1911, the year after it was published) Margaret Deland surprised readers with an awesome woman industrialist, an owner/manager of an iron-works, who possesses a genius for making money which is the equal of any man's in American fiction. Deland tries to be firm in her condemnation of Sarah Maitland, who neglects her children in her passion for work, but the book succeeds instead in giving its title-character mythic stature. Against a midnight backdrop of flames, smoke, and molten ore, Sarah, in heavy boots and wide-hemmed skirts, strides majestically through her iron-yards with each of her children in two of the book's crucial scenes; and she dies the death of a hero, holding on to life for days after being wounded while supervising rescue work in the yards in the wake of a horrible accident. If her life is finally repudiated by Deland because of her failure as a mother, her success as a capitalist is still impressive.

Less literal and therefore even closer to what Wharton does in *The Custom of the Country* is Frances Hodgson Burnett's 1906 best-seller about capital, *The Shuttle*. As a matter of fact, Burnett's novel has all the appearance of having been written to attract the audience Wharton landed with *The House of Mirth*, a big best-seller the year before Burnett's book came out, and it is very possible that Wharton knew the novel and made *The Custom of the Country* in some ways a response to it. Burnett's title refers to the fast steamers used by the very rich at the turn of the century to make rapid transatlantic crossings—jetting, so to speak, with great frequency from New York to fashionable European watering holes and then back again. But even if her title is realistic, her heroine, Betty Vanderpoel (the last name needs no gloss), in contrast to the heroine in Wharton's best-seller, Lily Bart, is pure fantasy—a flawless New Woman who possesses limitless wealth, beauty, courage, and freedom.

Setting out alone to rescue her sister from a tyrannical British nobleman she made the mistake of marrying, Betty Vanderpoel knows no fear. She explains to one of her amazed shipmates, "Women have found out so much. Perhaps it is because the heroines of novels have informed them. . . . I believe it is years since a heroine 'burst into a flood of tears.' It has been discovered, really, that nothing is to be gained by it." She adds: "Whatsoever I find at Stornham Court, I shall neither weep nor be helpless. There is the Atlantic cable, you know."[9] Betty hardly needs it. Single-handed, she finds her sister, restores her to health and hope, and uses her vast Vanderpoel wealth to completely do over the shabby baronial manor that has been timid Rosalie's prison (the project makes one think of Undine, who is always wanting to re-do heirlooms, while the image of imprisonment that the book is built on brings to mind Anna Leath's entombment at Givré as well as Undine's at Saint-Désert, the ancestral home of her third husband, Raymond de Chelles).

From start to finish *The Shuttle* is an entertaining escapist novel, an adventure fantasy for women with gothic trimmings. But it is also an accolade to American capitalism. Burnett's heroine declares of herself: "I am of the fighting commercial stock, and, when I see a business problem, I cannot leave it alone, even when it is no affair of mine."[10] Betty Vanderpoel, who we are told closely resembles her father, embodies in a woman the American myth of high morality, fearless individualism, and unlimited monetary success.

Wharton's capitalist heroine, in contrast, is no such fantasy creature. Undine is selfish and shrewd, the only one of Wharton's early heroines to deal successfully (that is, to her advantage) with economic and social reality; and she does so precisely because she is not virtuous. She is beautiful, she is clever, she is eager to be prominent within the structure of American society, and the way she achieves her goal is by playing—and playing to the hilt—a very old feminine game: snaring men as husbands. She is closer in type to Chaucer's Wife of Bath than she is to Burnett's romanticized capitalist

112

do-gooder Betty Vanderpoel. As Wharton makes clear through her spokesman Charles Bowen, the world has not really changed. For all the excitement about the New Woman in America at the turn of the century, for all the anxiety expressed in a character like Margaret Deland's Sarah Maitland, and for all the optimism fantastically caught up in a character like brave Betty Vanderpoel, what—this novel asks—has really changed? Divorce has made it easier to switch alliances, that is true. But women—even dashing young New Women like Undine and her friend Indiana—still live through men. In Wharton's view the woman who wants to make it to the very top of the American pyramid still has only one route: confederate with a man already up there, or one on the way. There is nothing "new" about this. Undine is an utterly modern American woman, and her story is ancient.

She decides to marry Ralph Marvell because, she thinks, as a member of the most elite stratum of the leisure class, he represents the apex of her social ambitions. Given their different temperaments and backgrounds, however, his attraction to Undine seems less understandable. Of course she is beautiful and vital. But why are even "her crudity and her limitations . . . a part of her grace and her persuasion" (p. 83)? The answer lies in the challenge Undine poses for Ralph, another in the growing ranks of Pygmalion figures in Wharton's fiction. A would-be artist who has never been able to finish a single work, he sees Undine as raw material for his creative impulse. He worries that her "virgin innocence" (ironically, she has already been married and divorced) will be corrupted by another and less idealistic artist, Popple, whose "vulgar hands were on it already—Popple's and the unspeakable Van Degen's! Once they and theirs had begun the process of initiating Undine, there was no knowing—or rather there was too easy knowing—how it would end!" (p. 82). Ralph wants to initiate her himself. "To save her from Van Degen and Van Degenism" therefore becomes the mission he romantically envisions for himself: "he seemed to see her like a lovely rock-bound Andromeda, with the devouring monster Society careering up to make a mouthful of her; and himself whirling down on his winged horse—just Pegasus turned Rosinante for the nonce—to cut her bonds, snatch her up, and whirl her back into the blue . . . " (pp. 82, 84; Wharton's ellipsis).

Even after four unhappy years of marriage, Ralph, still considering it his task to shape and improve Undine's character, is full of rationalizations: "After all, she was still in the toy age; and perhaps the very extravagance of his love had retarded her growth, helped to imprison her in a little circle of frivolous illusions. But the last months had made a man of him, and when she came back [from Europe] he would know how to lift her to the height of his experience" (p. 309). Accustomed to women who "yielded as a matter of course to masculine judgments" (p. 178), Ralph assumes that Undine wants to be lifted and will adopt his unostentatious way of life, his taste for reserved people, and his educated aestheticism. He assumes, in other words, that she wants to become a supportive, emotionally and intellectually dependent wife— both the object and the nurture of his creativity. Undine, however, wants to serve neither as his impressionable pupil nor his muse, and Ralph must eventually abandon the project. His wife simply will not adopt his values, especially his belief in the innate passivity of female human nature.

Undine's idea of marriage Thorstein Veblen captures perfectly when he describes the function of the rich man's wife, who should be "supported in idleness by her owner. She is useless and expensive, and she is consequently valuable as evidence of pecuniary strength." He explains that "the reason for the more extreme insistence on a futile life for this class of women than for the men of the same pecuniary and social grade lies in their not only being upper-grade leisure class but also at the same time a vicarious leisure class. There is in her case a double ground for consistent withdrawal from useful effort." In short: "In the ideal scheme, as it tends to realize itself in the life of the higher pecuniary classes . . . attention to conspicuous waste of substance and effort should normally be the sole economic function of the woman."[11] Mrs. Ralph Marvell would have no quarrel whatsoever with Veblen's description of the "ideal scheme." Her problem is that Ralph does not have the kind of money or attitudes that will allow her to realize that ideal.

As important as the relative poverty that limits her opportunities for conspicuous consumption, Undine also resents Ralph's Pygmalion attitude toward her, his subtle attempts to mold and upgrade her values. Before they marry, when he intimates that Popple's portraits are vulgar, she beings to resist Ralph's mentorship; and when he implies that he should choose her friends for her on their honeymoon, she is astonished, and then defiant. Alone in Europe a few years later, Undine thinks about that honeymoon summer when

there had been no child to hamper their movements, their money anxieties had hardly begun, the face of life had been fresh and radiant, and she had been doomed to waste such opportunities on a succession of ill-smelling Italian towns. She still felt it to be her deepest grievance against her husband; and now that, after four years of petty household worries, another chance of escape had come, he already wanted to drag her back to bondage! (pp. 282–83)

Undine's taste may need educating, but that is beside the point. She married in order to be displayed, not educated and hidden away in elegant seclusion like Ralph's mother or his cousin, Clare Van Degen. Consequently marriage with Ralph seems like "bondage" to her; she feels "imprisoned" (p. 245); she wants to "escape" from him.

Divorced from Ralph and deserted by Peter Van Degen, with whom she has had a brief miscalculated affair (it did not produce the marriage she had counted on), Undine experiences an obscurity far worse than the attention she resented from Ralph. She tries to create a life for herself as a single woman living abroad but fails because, without her married name, she has no identity of value to society. "Her new visiting-card, bearing her Christian name in place of her husband's, was like the coin of a debased currency testifying to her diminished trading capacity" (p. 361). Unmarried, she has no social status and nothing to do. Worse yet, when she returns to New York to live with her parents and attends the opera, society so obviously "cuts" her as a divorcée and Van Degen's former mistress that her first reaction upon return to the hotel is "immediate submission to her father's will" (p. 378); she agrees to send back the pearls Van Degen gave her. Normally defiant, Undine is so humiliated that, thinking in terms of the "pathetic allusions to woman's frailty" she has picked up from her novel-reading (evidently she has not read the same novels Betty Vanderpoel has), she considers her father "heroic" and depends for the moment on his rather than her own judgment (p. 376). Wharton's point is important. As a single woman, Undine is unrecognized, even ostracized; and she consequently grows spiritless and insecure. She must marry again in order to have identity itself, much less power.[12]

At first Undine thrives as the wife of Raymond de Chelles, Ralph's successor. "Her husband was really charming (it was odd how he reminded her of Ralph!), and after her bitter two years of loneliness and humiliation it was delicious to find herself once more adored and protected. The very fact that Raymond was more jealous of her than Ralph had ever been—or at any rate less reluctant to show it—gave her a keener sense of recovered power" (p. 480). This happiness is very short-lived. Even on their honeymoon Raymond dictates where she may go and with whom she may associate, and he expects her "to give a circumstantial report of every hour she spent away from him" (p. 481). His lovely jealousy, as Undine comes to realize too late, is not a sign of affection but of power. As Charlotte Perkins Gilman says in *The Man-Made World* of the limitations traditionally set on women (and Raymond is, if nothing else, a traditionalist), "the dominant male, holding his women as property, and fiercely jealous of them, considering them always as *his*, not belonging to themselves, their children, or the world, has hedged them in with restrictions of a thousand sorts."[13] It is not surprising that Wharton devotes little space to Raymond de Chelles; it takes little space to show that the "charming" Raymond is simply a nightmarish exaggeration of Undine's previous husband.

He has such a strong sense of proprietorship and cherishes such a suffocating ideal of passive femininity that Undine finds herself virtually entombed in his château, appropriately named Saint-Désert. There her "enforced seclusion" (p. 492) is relieved only by rare visits from dull relatives; Raymond lacks both the cash and the philosophy that would allow her to occupy herself with conspicuous consumption. Instead, the sole activity permitted her in this extremely conservative but nevertheless completely conventional environment is needlework. As Anna Garlin Spencer, following Veblen's lead, emphasizes in *Woman's Share in Social Culture*: "the lady must not earn money; she must not be a producer of any values not included in domestic and social occupations as outlined in the 'theory of the leisure class.' . . . Fine needlework; decorative weaving; 'arts and crafts' in reminiscent play-work; illuminating or binding books that only wealth can own or preserve"—these activities, plus a few more that recall the social arts in which Lily Bart was so well-trained, define the lady's realm.[14] Missing the point of Wharton's satire, one critic cites Undine's contempt for needlework as evidence of her moral poverty: "Next [after Ralph] is Raymond de Chelles, a French nobleman of 'simplicity and intelligence' who mistakes Undine for a beautiful candid American girl. But of course she hasn't inherited the dream of all the ages [woman as man's elevating moral force: especially the symbol for him of American idealism], merely the materials—energy and ambition and limitless egoism. This marriage bores her because she cannot adapt herself to the role required of 'the ladies of the line of Chelles,' who sit 'at their needlework on the terrace.' "[15] Certainly Undine *should* be bored with her restricted life at Saint-Désert. The fact that she is a highly flawed character does not make Raymond or his concept of a wife's role admirable; and we should no more wish that Undine could adapt to such a dreary life than we should lament her not having "inherited the dream of all the ages"—a male fantasy that casts woman in the impossible role of nymph/ nun cultural messiah. (Not surprisingly, there is no such idealized, redemptive American girl in Wharton's fiction.)

In her marriage to Ralph, and in this one to Raymond, Undine entered the relationship expecting to be placed on triumphant public display—modeling fabulous gowns, being seen dining leisurely at the finest restaurants, shuttling back and forth across the Atlantic, sporting jewels that would be written up on society pages from New York to Apex—only to find that her third husband, like her second (but with none of his tolerance) abhors publicity: he belongs to a very special subclass that prides itself on its *in*visibility. As if that weren't bad enough, compounding Undine's misery is Raymond's loss of interest in her because she will not acquiesce in his will. Although she resolves to "cultivate all the arts of patience and compliance" to win him back (p. 496), she cannot carry off the role of submissive wife—for which she is ingeniously punished by Raymond's refusing to sleep with her. Childless, she steadily loses status within the French family structure, the basis of power in French society. For a while she fights back—tormenting her mother-in-law, buying extravagant clothing, arguing with Raymond. But she develops "the baffled feeling of not being able to count on any of her old weapons of aggression. . . . A blind desire to wound and

destroy replaced her usual business-like intentness on gaining her end" (pp. 527–28). This is Undine's nadir. The almost
literal imprisonment she suffers at Saint-Désert erodes her
confidence in her own power and rectitude; and it brings out
in her a conscious viciousness, a desire to wound. She reacts
to entrapment as would any healthy, active creature: she
becomes demoralized, mean, and desperate. The wonder is
not that she contemplates selling the Chelles's ancestral
tapestries, but that she does not do so.

In 1907, six years before *The Custom of the Country*
appeared (but only one year before the novel was begun),
Wharton published a finely chiseled novella very much in the
Jamesian mode, *Madame de Treymes*, which shows how
powerful an opponent Undine overcomes in freeing herself
from Raymond de Chelles and his family. In this earlier story
Madame de Malrive, formerly Fannie Frisbee of New York
City, manages to obtain a separation from a similarly repulsive French husband but never from his despotic family.
They agree to the divorce that will enable her to remarry, but
they do so only because, unbeknownst to her or her future
husband, remarriage would automatically prohibit her from
keeping her son by Malrive. In fact, the family secretly con-
nives for divorce so that they can appropriate the son. (Separated from Malrive, Fannie is entitled to legal custody of the
boy; remarried, she would have no rights.) To show how
indomitable the solidarity of the French family is, Wharton
makes Malrive's sister, Madame de Treymes, who is Fannie's
one friend and defender, the family's instrument in the deception. To her credit, though she does the family's bidding by
encouraging Fannie to divorce, Madame de Treymes betrays
their motive—theft of the boy—before it is too late; and Fannie does not divorce Malrive and remarry. It is a sad victory,
however. To keep her child she must sacrifice her own happiness and all dreams of immediate independence from the
Malrives. Undine would probably not make the same choice,

but then that is conjecture. Faced with the same type of ruthless domestic tyranny but with no child at stake, she defies French custom and leaves Raymond de Chelles without one regret.

Undine is not admirable, of course. But neither is any other character in *The Custom of the Country*, Raymond de Chelles and Ralph Marvell included. To attribute Ralph's suicide to Undine's Circe-like destructiveness is to ignore the self-pity and fatuous self-sacrifice that motivate it. "He said to himself: 'My wife . . . this will make it all right for her . . .' and a last flash of irony twitched through him" as he pulled the trigger (p. 474; Wharton's ellipsis). Both Ralph and Undine have been playing the same game of trying to change the other person; put crudely, Ralph is an exceptionally poor loser. Similarly, to deplore Undine's abuse of her son as either an irrelevance or an "acquisition" (p. 478)—the book plainly encourages sympathy for the boy—should not obscure the fact that she treats him as his beloved stepfather, Raymond, treated her. That by no means excuses her behavior, but it does place it in context. And within the commercial context of this novel Undine's failure as a mother emphasizes Wharton's contention that the social system, much like Wall Street, is designed to promote the success of precisely the most callous, rapacious people. Concern for others and tenderness are weaknesses in the "jungle" of social, no less than economic, competition. (Given Wharton's fondness for mythology, it is likely that she plays with the idea here that the undine, according to myth, can acquire a soul only by marrying a mortal and bearing a child. Wharton's Undine remains soulless even in maternity, suggesting perhaps that the mortal world that inseminates her has no soul to bestow. If so, her lack of maternal concern, figuratively as well as sociologically, accentuates the culture's as much as her own inhumanity.) Moreover, even as we recognize that Undine is a terrible mother, we should ask: in this book who, in her own way at the over-solicitous other end of the spectrum, is not? Mrs. Spragg, Mrs. Marvell, and the Marquise de Chelles dote on their children (and look at them: Undine, Ralph, Raymond) with a vested devotion only somewhat less selfish than Undine's neglect of her child. No mother in *The Custom of the Country* would win any awards.

Even Undine's two most reprehensible actions Wharton takes care to place in context. Undine ignores the cable about Ralph's illness because she believes, as is plausible, that his mother and sister, who spend their lives protecting him and are always manufacturing sentimental terrors, would think nothing of alarming her as a device to bring her back from Europe. Equally significant, Moffatt conceives and suggests Undine's scheme to extort annulment money out of Ralph by threatening to take their son away from him. I do not point these things out to exonerate Undine, but to emphasize how carefully Wharton implicates most of the characters in the central theme of human usury, especially as manifest in the business of marriage.

Undine's story stands in much the same relation to Lily Bart's, a saddening treatment of the marriage question, as one of Edith Wharton's own shining Panhard-Lavassors (the "motor" that swept trembling Henry James off with her on their whirlwind excursions of sightseeing) did to the horse-drawn barouche of quieter times. By 1913, with *Ethan Frome* and *The Reef* immediately behind her, and a few years before them *The House of Mirth* and *The Fruit of the Tree*, Edith Wharton knew exactly what she had to say about the business of marriage, and she was not at all timid on the subject. Whereas in *The House of Mirth* she delicately expresses her criticism of leisure-class marriage by dramatizing a sensitive, but only vaguely self-aware young woman's fear of becoming some man's property within marriage, in *The Custom of the Country* Wharton adopts a bolder strategy. She creates in her protagonist an ambitious young woman who not only accepts the commercial nature of marriage but is also eager, as the image of a warrior queen emphasizes, to triumph by means of it—in the vernacular, eager to make a "killing." The stock market parallels are more than decoration. Endowed with a cunning business sense, Undine makes marriage her business in life. She speculates in husbands just as husbands speculate in stocks, and she is skillful at it. True, she makes a couple of investments that turn out badly: she did not understand that both Ralph and Raymond belong to the stable, aboriginal leisure class of their native countries and therefore desire a wife who, in Veblen's terms, will display conspicuous leisure for a small, exclusive group of people rather than conspicuous consumption for the benefit of the masses.[16] But she is smart enough to "unload" in each case. Consequently she is able to make a profitable deal in the end by remarrying Elmer Moffatt, her first husband, who, as a nouveau-riche multimillionaire, shares her belief that she should devote her life to conspicuously spending his money as vivid, public proof of his wealth and power.

Undine Spragg is no more exploitive than the culture that produced her. Instead of rejecting marriage because it is a usurious arrangement or enduring a restrictive marriage and thereby accepting failure, Undine—like an ambitious man changing jobs until he finds the "right" one—regards marriage as a commercial enterprise and, in fact, goes the system one better by viewing men as *her* possessions: she coolly gives "a smile of possessorship to Ralph" at the opera and, in Paris with Raymond, she "enjoyed going about with her husband, whose presence at her side was distinctly ornamental" (pp. 97, 507). There is a genius to Wharton's ironic strategy. What better way to expose how exploitive and demeaning leisure-class marriage is for wives than by placing men in the belittling role usually reserved for women? The book implicitly asks why, if it is distasteful to see a woman regard a man as an acquisition, is the reverse not equally true?

A character like Undine is rooted in two worlds. When Wharton's friend Bernard Berenson suggested that the names she gave Undine Spragg and her friend Indiana Frusk were unbelievable, Wharton laughed: "*Naïf enfant*. And how about Lurline Spreckels . . . and Florida Yurlee, two 'actualities' who occur to me instantly? As for similar instances, the 'Herald' register will give you a dozen any morning."[17] However, Undine not only brings to mind America's Lurline Spreckelses and Florida Yurlees; she also, because of her third marriage, calls up Consuelo Vanderbilts and Anna Goulds, envied American princesses whose glamorous marriages to titled Europeans—the Duke of Marlborough and Count Boniface de Castellane—seemed perfect fairy tales until their alliances, like Undine's equally bad match, ended (in 1912 and 1906) in ugly separations and divorce. First in Anna Leath's marriage to Fraser Leath in *The Reef* and then one year later in Undine's marriage to Raymond de Chelles in *The Custom of the Country* (and, as we will see, once again a few years later in Ellen Olenska's awful marriage to Count Olenski in *The Age of Innocence*), Wharton argues that bad as American marriages may be, tradition-bound aristocratic European ones can be worse. The higher up the social scale in Europe, the more historically dictated the marriage is likely to be, and hence the more restrictive for women. Wharton sympathizes with some of Undine's discoveries. Despite seductive press given the subject at the turn of the century, marrying into an old European house and title was not, in Wharton's view, an enlightened thing to do.

As a young American woman whose goal is to reach the very top of the American social ladder, Undine must climb through marriage: attachment to the right man is her only means of ascent; there is no independent route. She must agree to trade herself in marriage. (The option taken by the Princess Estradina—being married in name but not in practice—is clearly European not American.) Undine has two alternatives. Like Clare Van Degen, Laura Fairford, and Ralph's mother, she can conform to an old-fashioned ideal of acquiescent femininity and thus perpetuate the aboriginal leisure-class ideal of feminine self-effacement and conspicuous leisure displayed within a narrow circle. Or she can emulate the aggressive opportunism of her girlhood friends, Indiana Frusk and Mabel Blitch: she can marry new money and express her ambitious nature vicariously but publicly as the ostentatious spender of her husband's millions. By any standard, neither wifely role is attractive, for both designate the woman her husband's property, his chattel. As Elmer Moffatt, not yet totally financially successful, puts it when asked if he plans to marry: "Why, I shouldn't wonder—one of these days. Millionaires always collect something; but I've got to collect my millions first" (p. 419). Undine is not an admirable character because, within marriage as it is defined in this novel, there is for women no admirable way to accept or escape the collected state. To submit to it is to become a masochistic, self-effaced Clare Van Degen. To escape it one must apparently be a callous, profiteering Undine Spragg Moffatt Marvell de Chelles Moffatt—a woman as ruthless and exploitive as the culture she mirrors.

In her memoir, A *Backward Glance* (1934), Wharton recalled how Henry James "often bewailed to me his total inability to use the 'material,' financial and industrial, of modern American life. Wall Street, and everything connected with the big business world, remained an impenetrable mystery to him." Wharton had to admit that her old friend was right about himself: "The attempt to portray the retired financier in Mr. Verver, and to relate either him or his native 'American City' to any sort of concrete reality, is perhaps proof enough of the difficulties James would have found in trying to depict the American money-maker in action."[18] Wharton, in contrast, perfectly understood the modern American money-making scene, including the woman's stock market of marriage and divorce. The incidence of divorce was rising sharply in America, of course, when *The Custom of the Country* appeared;[19] and among the culprits commonly cited was the ambitious modern woman supposedly produced by the Woman Movement. Anna B. Rogers's *Why American Marriages Fail* (1909), for instance, attacks feminism and its self-centered New Woman for the alarming increase in divorce, which promised in her view, as in many others, to destroy the family in America. A little more than a decade later Edith Wharton would be agreeing; but not when she wrote *The Custom of the Country*. When she told Undine's story, it was still marriage, not divorce, that roused her cynicism.

The War

By 1915 Europe but not America was at war, and Orison Swett Marden, author of *Keeping Fit*, *The Optimistic Life*, and *He Can Who Thinks He Can*—not to mention *Cheerfulness* and *An Iron Will* (and the list of inspirational "Marden Books" runs much longer)—declared in *Woman and the Home*:

Although we are now witnessing one of the most brutal and bloody wars in history, nevertheless muscle and brutality are pretty nearly through in their attempt to govern the world. They have had their innings, and must soon wholly depart from the world's stage. Brain, reason, and judgment are rapidly supplanting them. The women are beginning to think, and their thinking is bringing them freedom, and as a consequence advancing the cause of all humanity. As long as woman was kept in ignorance she was kept in subjection, but knowledge has cut the shackles which bound her and she is rapidly thinking and working herself out of the semi-bondage in which she has so long been held. More and more she is coming to her own, to that perfect equality with man which is her birthright. Instead of walking behind him, in his shadow, as formerly, the woman of the future will walk beside man as is her right. Nothing is more marked in the world of progress during the past twenty-five years than the gradual loosening of the grip of man upon woman. Education is emancipating her. For the first time in history women in general have gotten a taste of freedom. They are feeling their power, the vast possibilities that lie ahead of them in the new civilization, and never again will they consent to their old-time slavery.[1]

Marden's book, one and a half decades into the twentieth century, expresses exactly the type of feminist optimism that Edith Wharton had been quarreling with for ten years. He announces that "the outlook is bright." Education and jobs are freeing women and promoting their self-development at unprecedented rates. "There will be no more female parasites," he says; "no more leaners, trailers, or dependents. . . . The great new woman movement is rapidly creating feminine leaders, organizers, captains, and generals of social campaigns. . . . They have exploded the idea that while there are a thousand vocations open to half the race there is practically only one—*i.e.*, marriage and motherhood—or at most a trifling few, open to the other."[2]

Intellectually, rhetorically, Marden is right. The Woman's Building at the 1893 Exposition; the new scholarship about women (as well as the lives and personalities of the new scholars themselves); the increased numbers of young women visible in the commercial sector, especially in sales and clerical work; the popularity of the New Woman in fiction and the graphic arts—all point to important changes in both the real and imagined status of women in America. Nevertheless, nothing, according to Edith Wharton, all of whose long fiction from *The House of Mirth* in 1905 to *The Age of Innocence* in 1920 takes up the woman question, nothing points to the demise of marriage as woman's one vocation.

Lily Bart says of marriage in Wharton's first full-length novel on the subject, "Ah, there's the difference—a girl must, a man may if he chooses,"[3] and this law governs woman's world in every one of Wharton's books about life before the 1920s. Neither Lily Bart at the top nor Mattie Silver at the bottom is in any way prepared and able to support herself in the world. Nor are Justine Brent and Sophy Viner— thoroughly modern, New Women—any better able to escape the parasitism Marden so happily sees disappearing. Even Undine does not escape; she simply does not mind the setup and makes the most of it, manipulating men to her advantage, as "clever," successful women have done immemorially. And Wharton's next two novels, one published during the war that

Marden dismisses too easily in 1915 and the other immediately following it, *Summer* (1917) and *The Age of Innocence*
(1920), do not alter her argument. Spanning fifty years of
American life, they show two very different American
women, Charity Royall and Ellen Olenska, rebelling against
age-old marital and sexual taboos, and failing. Surfaces might
be changing for women in Wharton's opinion; realities—
America's Orison Swett Mardens notwithstanding—were
not.

By the time Europe began fighting, Wharton's argument on
the woman question was fully matured, and the initial effect
of the war was simply to make her think even harder and more
deeply about her native land, almost as an anthropologist
thinks about strange, distant cultures. Economic dependence, sexual repression, the double standard, proprietary
marriage—these remain the facts Wharton stresses about
woman's lot in *Summer* and *The Age of Innocence*, much as
she had in *The House of Mirth* or *The Fruit of the Tree*. What
her argument does, however, is grow richer and more probing, incorporating analysis of prehistoric patriarchal fears
and customs into her realistic and highly historic fictions
about America. A few years after the war, as we will see in the
novels she published after *The Age of Innocence*, the very
foundation of her argument would change drastically. But
during and immediately following the war her thoughts on the
woman question remained consistent. She cast her analysis
first into primitive contemporary New England, expanding on
the start she made in *Ethan Frome*, and then into equally
primitive old New York; and she found in both worlds the
same ancient sexual politic. The American dream of personal
liberty does not apply to women, whose reality in both of
these books is slavery; Wharton's heroines are owned by
men. In *Summer* Charity is bound in marriage to the paternal
guardian—named Royall—from whom she has always longed
for freedom; in *The Age of Innocence* Ellen Olenska, forbid-

den to free herself from Count Olenski's loathesome marital hold, is ceremoniously sent back to Europe, and to him.

During the fighting, Edith Wharton's labor on behalf of France was so remarkable that in 1916 she was made a Chevalier of the French Legion of Honor, an unprecedented distinction for a woman and one sparingly awarded to foreigners. She lived in Paris at the time, and her contribution to the war-effort was prodigious: she raised funds, organized relief for refugees, founded hospitals and hostels, created jobs for war widows and homeless women, wrote propaganda, took in orphans. She differed from many people in not underestimating the probable magnitude of the war and therefore threw herself into relief work even at the beginning of the fighting, concentrating very early on establishing what became known as "American Hostels for Refugees." She worked closely with a younger woman who was to become a dear friend, Elisina Royall Tyler, and by long distance with her sister-in-law and old friend Mary Cadwalader Jones, who acted as her liaison in America. Lewis summarizes how, even early in the war, near the end of 1915, when

the American Hostels celebrated their first birthday, Edith could announce the following results: 9,330 refugees had been assisted during the year, 3,000 of them on a permanent basis; 235,000 meals had been served, and 48,000 garments handed out; 7,700 persons had received medical care; jobs had been found for 3,400. The whole undertaking had cost $82,000 in the first year, and monthly expenses ran to $6,000. To Sara Norton, Edith reported with exhausted pride that she had collected more than $100,000 in the preceding twelve months.[4]

Edith Wharton worked so hard because she loved France, the capital of civilization in her opinion, and because the suffering of the victims of the war was intolerable to her. She was outspoken in her belief that the United States betrayed both civilization and the human race in refusing to enter the war, and her denunciations of the Germans, like those of many of her generation, became blood-thirsty.

Yet the two fictions she wrote directly about the war, *The Marne* (1918) and *A Son at the Front* (1923), lack power. The first is a slim piece of propaganda, no better and some would say worse than the hundreds of such items produced during the war years by many authors. Somewhat superior is *A Son at the Front*, which is a full-sized novel. But still it is an after-the-fact melodrama; next to a book such as Willa Cather's *One of Ours*, published one year earlier, in 1922, Wharton's novel is shallow, even boring. The relative failure of these books has to do with the fact that although, finally, the First World War affected Edith Wharton more deeply and radically than any other experience in her life, it did not change her immediately and it was not in her fiction about the war that its influence was felt. Instead, the impression that the war made on her was delayed and appears in her fiction about civilian American life in the 1920s. That long-range change in her attitudes was major, as I will explain in the next chapter. The short-range effect, although significant, was by comparison minor and appears in her two domestic novels about love and authority, *Summer* and *The Age of Innocence*, where she brought to the subject of trapped women greater passion and compassion than she had felt, or at least expressed, since *The House of Mirth*. Both *Summer* and *The Age of Innocence* are strongly felt books.

The image of Edith Wharton as a cold, selfish person is a hard one to dispel chiefly because it is in part true. She was shy with strangers and demanding even of her friends; she could be sharp-tongued on occasion, and she was rich—hers was a life usually cushioned from ordinary want and coarseness. Yet, and this is extremely important, she would not blind herself to suffering. One of her friends recalled how she "possessed, indeed was possessed by, a sense of compassion deeper and more authentic than I have seen in any other human being. . . . The knowledge that there was mitigable suffering in a particular man or beast was enough to unseal the spring of her pity and she was not content to give money alone, she was ready to submit to boredom and something close to disgust" if her labors could help relieve the situation.[5] She was moved almost beyond words by the refugees who stumbled into wartime Paris. She said in 1915 in *Fighting France*, a collection of essays addressed to Americans in the hope that the United States would soon come to the aid of France,

Wherever one goes, in every quarter and at every hour, among the busy confident strongly-stepping Parisians one sees these other people, dazed and slowly moving—men and women with sordid bundles on their backs, shuffling along hesitatingly in their tattered shoes, children dragging at their hands and tired-out babies pressed against their shoulders: the great army of the Refugees. Their faces are unmistakable and unforgettable. No one who has ever caught that stare of dumb bewilderment—or that other look of concentrated horror, full of the reflection of flames and ruins—can shake off the obsession of the Refugees.[6]

Certainly one function *Summer* served for Edith Wharton was temporary escape from such wartime horrors. Like *The Age of Innocence* three years later, the story about Charity Royall contains some affectionate memories of America that border on the idyllic. The Fourth of July celebration that draws Charity and Lucius Harney to Nettleton, Massachusetts, for instance, is a superb piece of nostalgic writing. The two young people ride the interurban trolley, eat in a colorful little outdoor restaurant, tour the lake on an excursion boat packed with other young men and women decked out like themselves in straw hats and thin cotton dresses, and the day ends with shimmering fireworks canopying the lake. The outing, like some of Charity's walks alone in the unspoiled Massachusetts countryside or her rendezvous

with Harney in a weather-beaten abandoned house decorated
with wildflowers sitting in Mason jars, lingers like an image
from an Impressionist's canvas. There is an intense Ameri-
canness about *Summer*, and then *The Age of Innocence* with
its archery matches on the lawn, that reveals the part of Edith
Wharton that was profoundly war-weary and homesick for a
simpler time and place—which even she, however, knew was
in large part mythic.

For, despite the nostalgia, *Summer* and *The Age of Innocence* are finally severe and radically critical books. They
study underlying social structures and ancient taboos that
buttress patriarchal attitudes and prohibit freedom for
women, repressing in particular sexual passion. As early as
"The Valley of Childish Things" in the mid-1890s Edith
Wharton had criticized the American male preference for an
infantile rather than an adult mate, but although she reiter-
ated the point in *The Fruit of the Tree* she did not fully inquire
into the sexual dynamic involved until she wrote *Summer* and
The Age of Innocence. Clearly the war encouraged Wharton
to think about human behavior and institutions at their most
basic level. Although Ethan's preference for Mattie in *Ethan
Frome* and George Darrow's for Sophy Viner in *The Reef*
begin to investigate male sexual desire and fear, which *The
Children* takes up directly in 1928, *Summer* first clearly
identifies as unhealthy and incestuous the father-daughter
model of sexuality favored by patriarchal society.

Summer is short and was written rapidly as relief for Edith
Wharton from the exhaustion of the war work she had taken
on. She had had the story in mind for several years before
writing it out, so, strictly speaking, the book is not a product
of the war. Yet in some ways the novel surely reflects Wharton's situation. After finishing *The Custom of the Country*
she set out to write a large novel, called "Literature," about
the development of a young man into an author. She could
not get very far on the book (in fact, never was able to com-

plete it); the war intruded and when she did take time for her writing, the story she found herself able to tell was not a young man's and not an artist's; it was unlettered Charity Royall's. R. W. B. Lewis has commented that, except for one short story, "The Refugees," Edith Wharton did not use her war experience in her fiction; and literally that is true. However, the problems faced by Charity—abandonment, unwed pregnancy, poverty, ignorance, the temptation to become a prostitute—are not at all distant from those Wharton saw young women confronting in wartime Europe, and Charity Royall, at one remove, might well be thought of in relation to Wharton's refugees. At the very least, her story almost certainly takes both a lot of its bitterness and a lot of its poignancy from what Wharton had been seeing and feeling in her strenuous relief work, which brought her face to face with more elemental questions about human nature and society than she had been accustomed to ask.

The heroine of her book, Charity Royall, is a born rebel. She is a social outcast who is poor, feels nothing but contempt for the hypocritical morality of respectable small-town America, separates sex and matrimony in her own mind and life, and looks on marriage as a threat to the independence she craves. "How I hate everything!" she twice says to herself at the opening of the novel,[7] and she has good reason for the sentiment. Charity, at seventeen, is the ward of a deteriorated old lawyer named Royall in a decaying rural Massachusetts crossroads named North Dormer. She herself is called "Charity" because she is the local charity case. She was born among outlaws who live on a mountain that looms over the hamlet, and North Dormer's citizens make it their civic duty to keep her reminded of her disreputable origins: "Charity Royall had always been told that she ought to consider it a privilege that her lot had been cast in North Dormer. She knew that, compared to the place she had come from, North Dormer represented all the blessings of the most refined civilization. Everyone in the village had told her so ever since she had been brought there as a child" (p. 11). Charity's father was a convicted killer; her mother an alcoholic; Mr. Royall rescued her from the mountain when she was very young and proceeded to have her "christened Charity . . . to keep alive in her a becoming sense of her dependence" (p. 24). Naturally she despises him, just as she does North Dormer and everything about her life there. Her sole ambition is to escape. Instead, she falls in love with a young architect who summers in North Dormer, becomes pregnant, is abandoned, and ends up married to Royall, the paternal guardian whose presumption of authority she has always rebelled against but must now endure for much, if not all, of the rest of her life.

Thematically, the book is Wharton's bluntest criticism of the patriarchal sexual economy. The final union between Charity and Royall is not merely depressing; it is sick. For seventeen years Mr. Royall was Charity's father. Yet when she was fifteen he came into her room in the middle of the night, drunk, and tried to seduce her, perhaps even rape her if she, like Lily Bart in a similar scene in *The House of Mirth*, had not managed to be cool and self-possessed. This is the man who marries Charity; and Wharton's combination of threatened rape and figurative incest anticipates what a later critic, psychologist Phillis Chesler, has called the "rape-incest model" of sexuality and marriage in America: "While most women do not commit incest with their biological fathers, patriarchal marriage, prostitution, and mass 'romantic' love are psychologically predicated on sexual union between Daughter and Father figures."[8] Indeed, the incestuous nature of patriarchal marriage is the largest, the enveloping, subject of *Summer*. Royall proposes to Charity: "As he stood there before her, unwieldy, shabby, disordered, the purple veins distorting the hands he pressed against the desk, and his long orator's jaw trembling with the effort of his avowal, he seemed like a hideous parody of the fatherly old man she had always known. 'Marry you? Me?' " Charity flings at him "with a scornful laugh. 'Was that what you came to ask me the other night [when he tried to seduce her]? What's come over you, I wonder? How long is it,' " she adds for good measure, " 'since you've looked at yourself in the glass?' " (p. 34). Just the thought of marrying this old man disgusts Charity; yet in the end she is Mrs. Royall.

If she is the most openly defiant of Wharton's heroines, Charity Royall is also the most openly sexual. "She loved the roughness of the dry mountain grass under her palms, the smell of the thyme into which she crushed her face, the fingering of the wind in her hair and through her cotton blouse. . . . She often climbed up the hill and lay there alone for the mere pleasure of feeling the wind and of rubbing her cheeks in the grass" (p. 21). Wharton uses such descriptions to emphasize Charity's loneliness in North Dormer, a place as bleak and remote as its name implies, but also to identify her immediate problem. Nature is the only lover available to Charity Royall. *Summer* opens in June with Wharton's orphan an emotionally starved, sexually awakening young woman who craves pleasure, abandonment, physical gratification, and love. But she knows no human being to whom she can respond erotically, which explains her real reason for wanting to escape. North Dormer disapproves of passion; and she therefore has no outlet for the affectionate, sensual side of her personality, except when she is alone in nature.

With Lucius Harney, however, the refined young architect who spends his summer in North Dormer sketching old houses, Charity for a while experiences sexual freedom. But when she becomes pregnant she can no longer ignore social attitudes. She must decide how to cope with the sanction against unwed motherhood and illegitimate children. Although she could persuade Harney to marry her out of duty, she instantly rejects the idea. She has no desire to punish either of them by taking "North Dormer's point of view. Distinctly and pitilessly there rose before her the fate of the girl who was married 'to make things right.' . . . Poor Rose Coles's miserable marriage was of the number; and what good had come of it for her or for Halston Skeff? They had hated each other from the day the minister married them; and whenever old Mrs. Skeff had a fancy to humiliate her daughter-in-law she had only say: 'Who'd ever think the baby's only two? And for a seven month's child—ain't it a wonder what a size he is?' " (pp. 234-35). Charity has no intention of letting the village judge and humiliate her; she refuses to acquiesce in its puritanical attitude toward extramarital sex, much less the double standard which punishes the woman more than the man (if him at all) and reminds her of her transgression to keep her contrite and obedient. To do so would be to conform to a code she does not respect and to admit guilt she does not feel.

Nor does abortion appeal to her. Charity is horrified when Dr. Merkle, the Nettleton physician who diagnoses her pregnancy, assumes that Charity wants to abort; and the casual offer of this slick woman doctor to place Charity, after the abortion, as a lady's companion in Boston does not for a minute interest her. Her brief love affair was a phenomenon as natural to Charity as the woods and fields she has always felt close to, and the very idea of abortion profanes her inmost reverence for all things vital and spontaneous.

Resolved not to force Harney to marry her, not to have an abortion, not to live on the mountain (which is as depraved as North Dormer is repressed), and not to stay in the village, Charity, who is like Mattie Silver in that she had never been trained in "any trade that would have given her independence in a strange place" (p. 159), can think of only one course of action: prostitution.

Vague thoughts of Nettleton flitted through her mind. She said to herself that she would find some quiet place where she could bear her child, and give it to decent people to keep; and then she would go out like Julia Hawes and earn its living and hers. She knew that girls of that kind [prostitutes] sometimes made enough to have their children nicely cared for; and every other consideration disappeared in the vision of her baby, cleaned and combed and rosy, and hidden away somewhere where she could run in and kiss it, and bring it pretty things to wear. (p. 261)

Of course, as a prostitute Charity would discover herself owned and even victimized by men. But, from her point of view, how much worse could that be than life in North Dormer as a woman "indoors, engaged in languid household drudgery" (p. 9) or life on the mountain where everyone is trapped in helpless squalor and women like her mother live and die in brute misery? The fact that prostitution, not an attractive alternative in itself, seems less objectionable to Charity than either way of life to which she has been exposed accentuates Wharton's social criticism: given the extremely limited set of female options known in North Dormer, which as a primitive place knows of no profession for women except "the oldest," even prostitution seems preferable to the life of repression and degrading dependence Charity dreads were she to stay in the town and marry. Desperate for a solution, she believes "that the shunned Julia's fate might have its compensations. There were others, worse endings that the village knew of, mean, miserable, unconfessed" (p. 106). The sad course of *Summer* shows how Charity not only fails to escape one of those worse endings but finally is forced to submit to one with the very person she seeks to escape, Royall.

Charity's aversion to her guardian may seem nothing but the exaggerated and unwarranted hatred of the young and healthy toward the old and beaten. Indeed, the primitive setting and deterministic overtones of *Summer* would encourage such a judgment, were Wharton not so clear in her criticism of Royall. Viewed by himself, he is pitiable: an edu-

cated man of reduced fortune whose desire for companionship is as hopeless in North Dormer as his professional
training is wasted. But one cannot view Royall by himself in
Summer. He appears as Charity's guardian, her self-
appointed father, and then as her husband; and the quasi-
incestuous nature of that marriage is critical. As Wharton
emphasizes by having him drunk at the time, his attempt to
seduce his ward reveals weakness rather than evil; and he
himself regrets the episode. But he regrets it for the wrong
reason. He is ashamed of his lust rather than of his assumption that, because he brought her down from the mountain,
Charity belongs to him to do with as he pleases. Royall, to be
sure, is no George Darrow or Raymond de Chelles; he does
not consciously think of Charity as a possession. Nor is he
totally selfish or by any means villainous. Wharton does not
hate this character. The old man marries Charity because he
is mortally lonely; he needs her and sincerely wants to help
her. Still, the fact that his paternalism has a benevolent side
does not free it from being repugnant, as Wharton underscores by making his marriage to Charity figuratively incestuous. And the union he forces on his foster child without her
willing consent implies incest to suggest the fact that American marriage itself symbolically is incestuous. As Wharton
can show clearly in this book because of its unsophisticated
milieu, the institution of marriage is at bottom a paternalistic
and unhealthy extension of the relationship between father
and daughter.

   The way in which Royall makes Charity his wife dramatizes
Wharton's point. He is able to maneuver his "daughter" into
marrying him only because her ordeal of hiking up the mountain, added to her pregnancy, has made her unusually weak
and childlike. She is temporarily so weary and demoralized
that she has become "apathetic" and acts "half unconscious-
ly" (p. 268). Therefore Charity follows "Mr. Royall as passively as a tired child" (p. 274). "She knew that where he was

there would be warmth, rest, silence; and *for the moment they were all she wanted*" (p. 273; emphasis mine). If this interlude of childlikeness strikingly contradicts Charity's normally self-reliant, rebellious nature, the fact that marriage will perpetuate this abnormal submissiveness is equally obvious. The prospect of marrying young Lucius Harney, a man she loved, was unattractive enough: "Instead of remaining separate and absolute, she would be compared with other people, and unknown things would be expected of her. She was too proud to be afraid, but the freedom of her spirit drooped. . . ." (p. 213; Wharton's ellipsis). How much worse then the reality of a quasi-incestuous marriage to Royall, her foster father whose offers of marriage she has twice rejected and the man who epitomizes the dull, repressive way of life she had hoped to escape.

Catatonic at her own wedding, Charity's macabre reaction to the ceremony betrays her secret horror. "The clergyman began to read, and on her dazed mind there rose the memory of Mr. Miles, standing the night before in the desolate house of the Mountain, and reading out of the same book words that had the same dread sound of finality" (p. 278). The wedding reminds her of her mother's funeral, which is one of the ugliest scenes in all of Wharton. While the minister, Mr. Miles, reads the burial service over the contorted body of Charity's mother (the woman's toothless mouth will not close and one of her bloated legs refuses to unbend at the knee), assorted mountain kin and friends bicker over the woman's one worn-out possession, a cookstove, before lowering her into a grave on a filthy mattress. Charity's association of the two rituals, the funeral and the wedding, has its depressing logic. For with this October wedding her spirit, in effect, dies. "For an instant the old impulse of flight swept through her; but it was only the lift of a broken wing" (p. 280). Without alternatives Charity can make no choices; she can take no action. Passive, she falls victim once again to her guardian's benevolently selfish and inescapable paternalism. He marries her against her will, which is temporarily paralyzed, and practically against her knowledge: "What have I done? Oh, what have I done?" she asks herself on her wedding night, which she spends in a deadly trance (p. 283). This grotesque exaggeration of conventional, patriarchal marriage serves as Charity's punishment for loving a man out of wedlock. Her paternal guardian-turned-husband says to his now acquiescent daughter-made-wife "You're a good girl, Charity," and she responds "shyly and quickly": "I guess you're good, too" (pp. 290–91). Like one of the dazed refugees Wharton daily pitied in Paris, Charity Royall is at last broken.

Early in *Summer*, before she meets Harney, Charity sits alone in North Dormer's shrine to the past, the dilapidated Hatchard Memorial Library, where she halfheartedly works only to earn enough money to get out of North Dormer. She winds her handwork around "a disintegrated copy of 'The Lamplighter' " (p. 14), and the image could not be more prophetic. Charity Royall, a fiercely independent and strong-willed young woman does not read Maria Susanna Cummins's nineteenth-century best-seller about the virtues of developing, even at great pain, a second nature of feminine submissiveness and passivity. But that is the survival lesson (minus the virtues) that is nonetheless forced upon her in her seventeenth summer. Although Charity, unlike Gertie in *The Lamplighter* (1854), refuses to comply with her society's norm of docile femininity, outright rebellion against the double standard proves futile. She ends where she began: as the lawyer Royall's unnatural dependent. Only this time, as his wife, she is legally bound to him, a man not only old enough to be her father but one who has in fact been, and will in effect continue to be, just that.

Cynthia Griffin Wolff has suggested that Edith Wharton was unconscious of the incestuous nature of the relationship between Charity and Royall in *Summer* yet conscious and in control of much the same human construct two years later in the fragment "Beatrice Palmato," an explicit description of sexual relations between a father and daughter.[9] Wolff says that "the incest motif per se does not figure prominently in *Summer*; it is not a 'bad' thing that Charity eventually marries lawyer Royall. Quite the contrary." She believes that Wharton was not saying anything objective when she has the father figure sexually threaten and later marry his adopted daughter, but was instead "unthinkingly" expressing her own sexual problems: "Instinctively, perhaps—unthinkingly (since the violated taboo is never brought to the surface of the novel and condemned)—Wharton has plunged back to her own crisis of the threshold once again, now to resurrect not the chilling, immobilizing, regressive passivity and dependence on Mother that had served as the basis for the horror in *Ethan Frome*, but its converse."[10] Actually, there is no need to appeal to psychoanalytical theories here because the "violated incest taboo" *is* brought to the surface in *Summer*. Wharton is very much in control of the story's deadly denouement. Her book ends in autumn, the season of impending death, and the last we see of Charity, who is still only in her teens, she is married to a man for whom she not only feels no physical attraction, but in fact finds sexually repulsive. It is as if Lily Bart found herself married to Gus Trenor, but worse. This man has literally been a father to Charity, she a daughter to him. Funereal imagery precedes and then intrudes on their marriage at the end of *Summer* because, no matter how well-intentioned Royall is, this union between "father" and "daughter" is unhealthy and marks the end rather than the beginning of Charity's passional life. Royall will probably be kind to Charity; and certainly Wharton asks us to pity the man and perhaps feel glad that Charity has not fallen into the hands of someone even more violent than the broken-down lawyer. But that is the most that can be said for this incestuous marriage, which dooms Charity Royall to perpetual daughterhood—a fate that Wharton surrounds with images of spiritual paralysis and death.

It is true that in contrast to *Summer*, the incest in the "Beatrice Palmato" fragment is literal and explicitly sexual, and Wharton does make the subject erotic. But it should be emphasized that she also makes it sinister. Beatrice Palmato's father makes love to her in a room fitted out like one in a commercial bordello (black fur rug, purple velvet pillows, pink-shaded lamps) and the lovemaking, though it is ecstatic for the daughter, is a cool exercise in sexual expertise, a display of power, for the father. He leads, she follows; he is in control, she is not. Wharton never took the story further than an outline, which she probably, as Wolff argues convincingly, wrote around 1919 (rather than as late as 1935, which is the date Lewis would ascribe),[11] but even the outline of the story leaves little mystery about Wharton's reason for wanting to tell the tale. Mr. Palmato, the outline says, has two daughters. Because of him the elder commits suicide at seventeen; his wife then goes mad and dies in an insane asylum; then Beatrice, the younger daughter, kills herself following her affair with her father. No matter how erotic the seduction scene in which Mr. Palmato has intercourse with his own daughter (and bear in mind that one can imagine a perfectly executed crime and not necessarily approve the deed), the finished story, unless Wharton had changed it radically, was going to present incest as an act that kills women. Mr. Palmato murders his wife and two daughters as surely as if he had taken an ax to them. To arrive at even the most speculative of conclusions about the "Beatrice Palmato" fragment (and any conclusion about an unfinished work must be speculative) it must be read in light of the story outline Wharton left with it, which includes no less than three deaths as a consequence of the father's incestuous relations with his daughters. (The name Beatrice, of course, also sheds light on Wharton's purposes by calling to mind Beatrice of Cenci, who was raped by her father and therefore murdered him.)

Of major importance on this whole subject of unhealthy sexual power is the visit Wharton made to North Africa as brief respite from the war in 1917, the same year that *Summer* was published (she had made a similar trip three years earlier, not long before writing *Summer*). For while she was in Morocco, Wharton saw for herself patriarchal sex pushed to its logical, primitive—and very depressing—extreme. She was accorded the rare honor of being able to visit an imperial harem in Marrakech, and her description of the experience in *In Morocco* (1920) shows how horrible she found the spectacle. The women she saw lived, in her opinion, in a gilt "prison," and all but one of them were mindless, severely arrested creatures. The "trivial dissimulations, the childish cunning, the idle cruelties of the harem" dismayed Wharton, even though she well understood their inevitability under the circumstances. The "languid" child-women were provided with no occupation to pass the time and absolutely no freedom; they were "beings imprisoned in a conception of sexual and domestic life based on slave-service and incessant espionage." She says that "in their stuffy curtained apartment they were like cellar-grown flowers, pale, heavy, fuller but frailer than the garden sort," and the whole unhealthy environment is one filled for women, according to Wharton, with melancholy. Here "both sexes live till old age in an atmosphere of sensuality without seduction" and children are badly brought up by inert women whose ignorance and immaturity men zealously cultivate and guard.[12]

It is completely consistent with Wharton's criticism of the patriarchy at this stage in her career that she emphasizes the absence of sexual passion in the harem, the supposedly most sexy of all male-oriented systems. For she knows, arguing it first in *Summer* and then in *The Age of Innocence*, that the free expression of female sexuality represents a profound threat to patriarchal power, and is therefore assiduously guarded against. Turned around: the most desirable wife in the eyes of the patriarchate (and marriage, of course, is the sine qua non of patriarchal power) is not sexual, whether she is one of many women in a harem in Marrakech, or Mrs. Lucius Harney in rural twentieth-century New England, or Mrs. Newland Archer in leisure-class old New York. Charity Royall and Ellen Olenska are both sexually vibrant, passionate women, and the men they love (and who love them) do not marry them. They marry their pale blonde antitheses. Lucius marries cool, virginal Annabel Balch; Newland marries May Welland. The dark women in both novels are rejected in favor of fair-haired child-women whose images and function recall the theme of Wharton's early parable, "The Valley of Childish Things": male fear of mature women.

War forces people to think about basic things, and one reality that Edith Wharton obviously thought about was fear. It is the subject of *The Age of Innocence*. Newland Archer and his fellow old New Yorkers are so afraid of Ellen Olenska, a sophisticated, sexually exciting woman, that they end up literally banishing her from New York. To be sure, their fear is not of the same quality that Edith Wharton, during the war, had seen daily—the acute terror of extermination; what the war could and did do to people's lives was very different from the neurotic apprehensions of sheltered old New Yorkers in the period Wharton baptized the Age of Innocence, the American 1870s. At the same time, however, the sexual fear that Ellen Olenska arouses in Newland Archer and his fellows is both deep and serious for, in the opinion of the people threatened, she places in jeopardy the very security of "civilization." Her presence upsets old New York's most basic principles of order and authority; and Wharton repeatedly uses anthropological terms and images in *The Age of Innocence*—elaborating for us "rituals" and "rites," referring to families as "tribes" or "clans," labeling Mrs. Manson Mingott the "grand Matriarch" of her line and comparing the Van der Luydens to tribal judges—to emphasize the way in which this book, lovely as it is, amounts to a sort of laboratory study of the fundamental, primitive attitudes that mold patriarchal aversion to the mature female.

The plot of Wharton's book is simple. On the eve of Newland Archer's engagement to May Welland, who is one of leisure-class old New York's perfect child-women, Ellen Olenska returns to New York; she has been living in Europe for ten years, the wife of a despotic minor nobleman, and she now plans to get a divorce. Society is shocked, as is Newland, but he is also captivated: he falls in love with Ellen, but marries May as he promised, and then asks Ellen to be his mistress. But the Countess Olenska, unlike naive Charity Royall, knows the consequences of illicit passion and, though unconventional about many things, has no illusion that she can violate the taboo against extramarital sex for women. She challenges Archer: "Is it your idea, then, that I should live with you as your mistress—since I can't be your wife?" He stutters:

"I want—I want somehow to get away with you into a world where words like that—categories like that—won't exist. Where we shall be simply two human beings who love each other, who are the whole of life to each other; and nothing else on earth will matter."

She drew a deep sigh that ended in another laugh. "Oh, my dear—where is that country? Have you ever been there?" she asked; and as he remained sullenly dumb she went on: "I know so many who've tried to find it; and, believe me, they all got out by mistake at wayside stations: at places like Boulogne, or Pisa, or Monte Carlo—and it wasn't at all different from the old world they'd left, but only rather smaller and dingier and more promiscuous. . . . Ah, believe me, it's a miserable little country!"[13]

Their story ends with Ellen Olenska being forced to return to Europe, and the book as a whole ends with a glimpse of Archer, widowed and twenty-five years older, sitting on a bench in Paris, looking up at Madame Olenska's windows but preferring to imagine rather than see her.

Ten years before Wharton's novel was published (and became an immediate best-seller) Emily Putnam had defined and studied, historically, the "conventional type of lady, who is distinguished from women at large by the number of things she may *not* do."[14]Wharton's heroine learns just how apt that definition is. An avid and intrepid reader who sees nothing wrong in leaving books scattered about her drawing room, where they are not supposed to appear, she brings from Europe a conception of the kind of salon atmosphere which makes life stimulating and gives it meaning, and she hopes to create that milieu in New York. She moves into a peeling stucco house on a vagabond block of West Twenty-third Street where "small dressmakers, bird-stuffers, and 'people who wrote' were her nearest neighbours" (p. 65) and amid the "vague pervading perfume" of her drawing room—it has "the scent of some far-off bazaar, a smell made up of Turkish coffee and ambergris and dried roses" (p. 69)—she tells astonished Newland Archer how much she enjoys living alone in her queer little house; she is baffled by the pressure on her to move: "I've never been in a city where there seems to be such a feeling against living in *des quartiers excentriques*. What does it matter where one lives? I'm told this street is respectable." When he replies that "it's not fashionable" she wonders aloud: "Fashionable! . . . Why not make one's own fashions?" (pp. 71–72). As her originality and her talent for improvisation reveal, Ellen is at heart an artist—an imaginative, passionate person, whose creative medium is her own life. That—in addition to her status as a would-be divorcée who wants to lead her life independently, much as a bachelor might—insures her clash with society. Old New York, like provincial North Dormer fifty years later, distrusts passion, intellectual and artistic no less than physical.

Edith Wharton remarked in *A Backward Glance* that "the

weakness of the social structure of my parents' day was a blind dread of innovation, an instinctive shrinking from responsibility,"[15] and the statement practically serves as a gloss for *The Age of Innocence*. The book looks back to the America of her parents' generation (she herself was only around ten at the time the novel is supposed to take place) as if to uncover the roots of repression still secretly nourishing modern American attitudes toward women. For Ellen Olenska is in many ways a New Woman available to America as early as 1870. She comes home to the United States because, in her own words, "I want to be free; I want to wipe out all the past" (p. 107). But she leaves America the guest of honor at "the tribal rally around a kinswoman about to be eliminated from the tribe" (p. 337). She is banished rather than welcomed, and the novel includes May Welland to illustrate why.

In *French Ways and Their Meaning*, a book of essays published in 1919, one year before *The Age of Innocence*, Wharton maintained that "like the men of her race, the Frenchwoman is *grown up*. Compared with the women of France the average American woman is still in the kindergarten." Wharton wrote this essay about "The New French Woman" during the war to increase American respect for French people and culture, and her praise for all things French is consequently extravagant. She says:

> The reason why American women are not really "grown up" in comparison with the women of the most highly civilised countries—such as France—is that all their semblance of freedom, activity, and authority bears not much more likeness to real living than the exercises of the Montessori infant. Real living, in any but the most elementary sense of the word, is a deep and complex and slowly-developed thing. . . . It has its roots in fundamental things, and above all in close and constant and interesting and important relations between men and women.[16]

In fact, as her fiction illustrates, women do not enjoy real equality with men in France or any part of Europe (*The Reef* and *The Custom of the Country* both argue the point, as will *The Mother's Recompense* and *The Gods Arrive* after *The Age of Innocence*). Women, do, however, have intellectual and some sexual freedom in France, and there is no infantilization of the sex like that in America which Wharton attacks in this essay and then shortly thereafter in *The Age of Innocence*. In it the conviction that America actually teaches women to remain childish shapes Wharton's characterization of May Welland much as it did Bessy Westmore in *The Fruit of the Tree* more than a dozen years earlier; and the cultural preference for May over Ellen reiterates Wharton's by-now familiar charge against the American patriarchy. She argues that it is a system deliberately designed to arrest female human nature.

May, we are told, has been "carefully trained not to possess . . . the experience, the versatility, the freedom of judgment" (p. 41) one needs in order to deal with adult life; she is "that terrifying product of the social system . . . the young girl who knew nothing and expected everything" (p. 40). She is still in the nursery. Like her mother, who has an "invincible innocence," she typifies the American woman described by the heroine of "New Year's Day," a story Edith Wharton wrote about the 1870's and included in her collection of four historical sketches, *Old New York* (1924): "Lizzie Hazeldean had long since come to regard most women of her age as children in the art of life . . . charming creatures who passed from the nursery to marriage as if lifted from one rose-lined cradle into another."[17] In *The Age of Innocence* other people must look out for May Welland's well-being and do her thinking for her. She is a precious human burden, the highest expression of the leisure-class's "nursery parody of life" (p. 182) and symbolic of its freedom from normal economic imperatives. America's answer to Chinese foot-binding, the child-woman May perfectly embodies her class's ideal of helpless femininity. She is a lovely human doll whose uselessness aggrandizes her owner's social standing, giving him the "glow of proprietorship" (p. 212) at the same time that her Diana-like virginity arouses "the passion of masculine vanity" for conquest and mastery (p. 44).

Appropriately, Archer marries May in "a rite that seemed to belong to the dawn of history" (p. 179); and, predictably, the ritual initiates him into the tribal mores rather than them both into any fuller experience of life. After only three months of marriage, this man (rather heavy-handedly named New-land) abandons his fledgling theory that women should be as free as men and reverts "to all his old inherited ideas about marriage. It was less trouble to conform with the tradition and treat May exactly as all his friends treated their wives than to try to put into practice the theories with which his untrammelled bachelorhood had dallied. There was no use in trying to emancipate a wife who had not the dimmest notion that she was not free; and he had long since discovered that May's only use of the liberty she supposed herself to possess would be to lay it on the altar of her wifely adoration" (p. 196).

Bessy Westmore and May Welland are sisters across the decades. Like the industrial society that produces her, Bessy is more hedonistic, materialistic, and careless of people and tradition than May. But only superficial manners and morals have changed in the intervening thirty years. Basically the two characters represent the same cultural phenomenon: the American child-woman who epitomizes her era's ideal femininity. The two characterizations emphasize that the ideal is a constellation of qualities adults enjoy in children: gaiety, innocence, ignorance, acquiescence, dependence, affectionateness, and a decorous spontaneity. But although childish traits including even greed and self-absorption can be charming in children (as Wharton rather clumsily tries to show in *The Children*), in an adult they can get oppressive. John Amherst and Newland Archer discover this. Why, then, Wharton poses the question in *The Age of Innocence*, does America produce the child-woman?

Newland Archer, apprehensive about his wedding night with May, provides the beginning of an answer when he reflects on May's limitations and feels "himself oppressed by this creation of factitious purity, so cunningly manufactured by a conspiracy of mothers and aunts and grandmothers and long-dead ancestresses, because it was supposed to be what he wanted, what he had a right to, in order that he might exercise his lordly pleasure in smashing it like an image made of snow" (p. 43). Newland is correct: the child-woman is created *by* women *for* men: she is manufactured in all her artificiality and ignorance of life because she is "supposed to be" what men want and by "right" shall have. She is, in other words, a male idea. And though Archer has doubts, the scheme must please most men, or at least those in power. For American society, as Edith Wharton portrays it, is resolutely patriarchal.

"Among our many naive misbeliefs," Charlotte Perkins Gilman had written in *The Man-Made World* (1911), "is the current fallacy that 'society' is made by women. . . . Men and women alike accept this notion; the serious essayist and philosopher, as well as the novelist and paragrapher, reflect it in their pages." Gilman analyzes the typical line of reasoning—to which Archer, though not Wharton, subscribes: " 'Society' consists mostly of women. Women carry on most of its processes, therefore women are its makers and masters, they are responsible for it, that is the general belief." She remarks, "We might as well hold women responsible for harems—or prisoners for jails. To be helplessly confined to a given place or condition does not prove that one has chosen it; much less made it. No; in an androcentric culture 'society,' like every other social relation, is dominated by the male and arranged for his convenience."[18]

Gilman's brief analysis helps explain, perhaps, how it is that many critics have failed to grasp the patriarchal structure of Wharton's "matriarchal" old New York. Widowed, Mrs. Manson Mingott indeed figures as the grand "Matriarch of the [Mingott] line" (p. 10). But she is second echelon. As Louis Auchincloss, one of the critics not taken in by the novel's smoke screen of supposed female power, points out: "Even old Catherine Mingott, the ancestress and dowager, known to an awed New York as 'Catherine the Great,' is not, in the last analysis, so very formidable. Her bluster and independence are little more than poses, and in the big decisions she is swayed by her son and her lawyer."[19] As her obese immobility emphasizes, she has no real freedom; she cannot even leave her house unassisted. Mrs. Manson Mingott is a refreshing but assimilated old eccentric whose figurehead power can be, and is, manipulated by men when necessary.

The head of the overall power structure in *The Age of Innocence*, Wharton makes clear early in the novel, is one man: Henry van der Luyden, the highest authority on morality and form and the supreme judge whose decrees are disseminated by Sillerton Jackson and Lawrence Lefferts (by no accident, both men). Wharton surrounds Henry van der Luyden with regal and religious imagery which shows that, although his wife has considerable influence as an intercessor, Mr. van der Luyden wields the power—his is the simple elegance that makes one think of "a reigning sovereign," his gesture that has "an almost sacerdotal importance" (p. 51). He pronounces with "sovereign gentleness" (p. 55) that New York shall not "cut" Ellen Olenska and, so long as he supports her—and only that long—the matrons countenance her. Thus society's apparently matriarchal structure functions as a useful substructure, as well as facade, in a culture firmly patriarchal. Of matriarchy Sir James George Frazer hypothesized in *The Golden Bough*, a book that Edith Wharton read with fascination: "In a state of society where nobility is reckoned only through women—in other words, where descent through the mother is everything, and descent through the father is nothing—no objection will be felt to

uniting girls of the highest rank to men of humble birth, even
to aliens or slaves, provided that in themselves the men
appear to be suitable mates."[20] Frazer's description of matriarchy finds its exact opposite in Wharton's remark about
leisure-class old New York's attitude toward humbly born
men: "If society chose to open its door to vulgar women the
harm was not great, though the gain was doubtful; but once it
got in the way of tolerating men of obscure origin and tainted
wealth the end was total disintegration" (p. 341). In *The Age
of Innocence* the male, not the female, line matters.

Given the patriarchal structure of American society, the
child-woman must represent a type of womanhood dear to
men; and, indeed, the conspiracy Archer senses does serve
male purposes: women teach other women to live within the
status quo. Hostility among women is an important factor in
this system, which is most clearly spelled out in *The Age of
Innocence* but operates in Wharton's other early novels as
well. Since it is frequently women who are charged with
keeping other women "in their place," often the enemies of
Wharton's heroines, toward whom they rightly feel hostile,
are not men; they are other women who have been taught to
act as the patriarchate's repressive agents, explicitly or implicitly. Rivalry and hostility between women are thus guar-
anteed, as in the cases of May Welland and Ellen Olenska or
Bessy Westmore and Justine Brent. Each twosome is made
up of a conventional and an unconventional woman, one the
unthinking product of patriarchal mores and the other a rebel
against them. While Wharton is more sympathetic with the
exceptional woman, the one who rebels, the emphasis she
puts on the conventional woman's being the victim of her
culture shows the political insight that informs her criticism.
She does not like May or Bessy, but she makes it clear that it
is how the culture has shaped them and set them up as
norms, rather than who they are intrinsically, that she
criticizes. In other words, the conspiracy that Archer senses

abuses women, not men. Hostility among women and the factitious child-woman originate in a patriarchal preference for wives who conform to a reassuring masculine ideal of feminine weakness.

The Fruit of the Tree ends with Amherst's preferring an imaginary Bessy to the real Justine. The Age of Innocence ends similarly with Archer's preferring May, dead, to Ellen Olenska, alive. He finds himself afraid of new experiences, trapped by memory and habit. "Something he knew he had missed: the flower of life" (p. 350); yet he would rather continue to miss out on life than dare meet Ellen again. Pathetically, he cherishes his memory of May (and Ellen) over the reality of seeing Ellen. (Likewise, at the end of The Fruit of the Tree, it should be remembered, it is not Bessy but his distorted recollection of her that Amherst loves.) Archer's timidity makes realistic sense: life does not repeat itself and Ellen might no longer like him. Wharton's point, however, is symbolic; and The Age of Innocence and The Fruit of the Tree, although published more than twelve years apart, conclude with the same idea. Memorializing the fair child-woman while fearing the dark adult, the once daring but basically conventional hero finally affirms his culture's preference in women. Despite an unhappy marriage, Newland Archer mythicizes May after her death, and he does so out of fear of the dark, "grown-up" woman.

Wharton would continue to think about this fear of the adult female throughout the 1920s, seeing in the flapper her worst fears surpassed: May Welland and Bessy Westmore look almost attractive compared to the "jazz-baby" America came up with after the war. As Wharton went on to demonstrate in The Children in 1928 (and The Children is the most interesting book to come out of the last decade of her career, even though it is not all that well written), an unbroken line existed from May Welland in the 1870s through Bessy Westmore in the early 1900s to the flapper in the 1920s.

Postwar America, to Wharton's dismay, would continue to manufacture and idolize the child-woman.

Although her deepest sympathies were shortly to realign, throughout the war and then on through the publication of *The Age of Innocence* and even a year or two beyond, Edith Wharton cared intensely about the question of freedom and self-fulfillment for women. Writing to Sinclair Lewis in 1921 at the beginning of his career, and the pinnacle of hers, she said of his 1920 novel, *Main Street*, which describes the killing vapidity of married life for one middle-class young housewife: "Your book and *Susan Lenox* (unexpurgated) have been the only things out of America that have made me cease to despair of the republic—of letters."[21] Thirteen years later she still considered David Graham Phillips's *Susan Lenox*, which was published in 1917, the same year as *Summer* (and by the same publisher), an "unjustly forgotten masterpiece." She grouped it with Howells's *A Modern Instance*, Grant's *Unleavened Bread*, Lewis's *Main Street* and *Babbitt*, the "best of Frank Norris" (what that is exactly she does not say), and Dreiser's *An American Tragedy*. These books she praised because they marked out an important new field in American literature, one that dealt with "the tragic potentialities of life in the drab American small town"[22]—a field or tradition, of course, to which she contributed as much or more than anyone with *Ethan Frome* and *Summer* and, indirectly, *The Custom of the Country*.

Just as important: *A Modern Instance, Unleavened Bread, Susan Lenox,* and *Main Street*—four of the six titles listed— are books that, although exhibiting a range of sympathies and arriving at very different conclusions, have in common a focus on the marriage question from a young woman's point of view. Significantly, of the group it is Phillips's novel that is politically the most radical and sophisticated, and his that Wharton, calling it a masterpiece, twice singled out as extremely important and well done. Howells's she wanted to

admire equally, but in her opinion "the incurable moral timidity which again and again checked him on the verge of a
masterpiece drew him back even from the logical conclusion
of 'A Modern Instance.' "[23]

Critics and readers have for so long associated Wharton
with Europe, with James, with the genteel tradition, with
everything but the resolutely American context she usually
wrote for, out of, and about, that her enthusiasm for Phillips's
muckraker may come as a surprise. The book covers the
years from seventeen to twenty-two in the life of a young
woman who, "illegitimate" by birth, chooses prostitution
over her other alternatives: marriage among the working
class or employment in a factory. Disease, filth, violent
crime, hideous overcrowding, abject hopelessness relieved
only by heavy drinking or opium (the first of which Susan
becomes addicted to) are the realities of tenement life. On top
of inhuman factory work that consistently paid so little that
the laborers, trapped like slaves, could never extricate themselves from their poverty, these conditions make it clear that
the only way out for a woman without family or a husband is
prostitution. And even that is far from a sure thing. As if in
mockery of Charity Royall's sweet vision of life in "the tender-
loin," surrounding Susan in every tenement she inhabits are
women in various stages of decay, physical and psychological, who will spend their lives working the streets at night
after working in the factories all day, yet between the two jobs
still never have the money or strength to get themselves out of
the slums.

Susan Lenox, after several years of streetwalking and factory exploitation, gets the chance to make a lucrative marriage. A man who was once her pimp is now a rich capitalist.
In a scene reminiscent of Simon Rosedale's proposal to Lily
Bart in *The House of Mirth* or prosperous Elmer Moffatt's
appeal to Undine in *The Custom of the Country*, Phillips's
Freddie Palmer says to Susan: "You were better born than I

am—you've had better training in manners and dress and all the classy sort of things. I've got the money—and brains enough to learn with—and I can help you in various ways. So—I propose that we go up together." Susan thinks the partnership a good idea but refuses to marry. She explains, "If I married you, I'd be signing an agreement to lead your life, to give up my own—an agreement to become a sort of woman I've no desire to be and no interest in being."[24] She feels no obligation to honor society's hypocritical code which calls sex sold in the church a woman's virtue and sex sold on the street, sin. Sex sold is sex sold in Susan Lenox's, and her author's, opinion; and how could anyone claim that marriage in its current state, as Charlotte Perkins Gilman had argued earlier in the century, was anything more than prostitution made respectable? Susan Lenox prefers not to sell herself in either the overt or the covert arrangement. She is glad to leave the street for good when she can; but she would return to it if she had to, Phillips makes obvious, before she would marry for support.

Wharton's enthusiasm for *Susan Lenox* is instructive. The book, like *Summer* and *The Age of Innocence*—novels very different in their surface texture but not their underlying social criticism—argues that marriage enslaves women. For Charity Royall, Susan Lenox, and Ellen Olenska marriage is the antithesis of the liberation they seek; it deprives them of the self-determination to which any adult human being in a supposedly free society is entitled.

Also instructive is the fact that, although Wharton had nothing but praise for *Susan Lenox*, a book that for its day is frequently lurid in the subject matter it treats, she disliked *The Jungle*. For as portraits of slum life and exposés of industrial exploitation the two men's books are very similar. The difference is that Phillips, like Wharton herself, applies no stock ideological solution to the problems he presents. Upton Sinclair's socialism Wharton found obnoxious, and told him so. When he appealed to her for support against the charge that his muckraker *Oil!* (1927) was "obscene," she readily responded: "I shall be glad if my name is of any use to you in freeing the novel from this unjust and ignorant aspersion." But she had to add concerning his politics, "I make this critique without regard to the views which you teach, and which are detestable to me."[25] Both her own fiction and her taste in others' show that Edith Wharton was not at all the insensitive, apolitical person that popular opinion and even many critics have painted her. From the wretched Bunner Sisters to Ethan Frome to Charity Royall, she expressed more than sympathy or vague compassion for the poor; she expressed anger that any human sensibility should be crushed and ground by poverty into the type of dumb, brute existence of which she (maybe because of her own privileged life) keenly felt the horror. Yet, like David Graham Phillips in *Susan Lenox*, Wharton in her novels through *The Age of Innocence* attempted no solutions. At her best she was a critic not a visionary.

Perhaps the explanation is logical and simple; on the issue of most concern to her—the issue of woman's life and liberty—she obviously believed that any "solution" would have to consist of revolutionary changes in men's, not women's, attitudes: in a patriarchy only the opinion of men matters. It is that simple. And not one of her books, including *Summer* and *The Age of Innocence*, which together bring to a close the Progressive Era phase of her argument with America, suggests that men in any way want, or have ever wanted, minor let alone revolutionary change.

Mothers and Flappers

"These four years have so much changed the whole aspect of life," Wharton said in the spring of 1918, "that it is not easy to say now what one's literary tendencies will be when the war is over."[1] Surely she could not have even guessed what did happen. After *The Age of Innocence*, which marks a sort of pause during which she applied to the decade of the 1870s the type of feminist social criticism that had worked from *The House of Mirth* through *Summer*, Edith Wharton turned her attention to the present, the 1920s, and wrote novels declaring motherhood woman's best and most fulfilling job in life.

For a number of years she was not fully aware of the change. With the war behind her (she thought) and a new decade firmly begun, Wharton confidently set about writing the kind of novel she had for twenty years come as close to perfecting as any writer of the Progressive Era: the sophisticated, realistic novel of social debate on the woman question. A typical Wharton novel was one that showed a young woman confronting marriage; that questioned national optimism about the New Woman and her supposed economic freedom; that forced its readers to think critically about romantic love, or prostitution, or the double standard, or the childishness of most grown women. And in the 1920s Wharton tried very hard to write these familiar sorts of books. First came *The Glimpses of the Moon* in 1922, which tells the story of a leisure-class young woman whose predicament is a cross between Lily Bart's and Undine Spragg's; Wharton's heroine, ill-equipped to support herself independently, turns her economic parasitism to advantage by capitalizing on the wealth of her friends. *The Mother's Recompense*, published three years later, in 1925, which was the same or very nearly the same time that *The Great Gatsby*, *The Sun Also Rises*, and *An American Tragedy* appeared (the last Wharton especially admired though she also liked *Gatsby* a great deal), seems in many ways a reworking and synthesis of *The Reef* and *The Age of Innocence*. As in *The Reef*, an older and a younger woman closely connected to one another (in this case they are mother and daughter) find themselves in love with the same man and, as in *The Age of Innocence*, the older woman is cruelly ostracized by American society. Finally, *Twilight Sleep* in 1927 attacks the middle-American boosterism that Wharton had earlier but less centrally taken on in *The Custom of the Country*, which served as an inspiration to Sinclair Lewis first in *Main Street* (1920) and then in *Babbitt* (1922), the novel he admiringly dedicated to Edith Wharton.

These novels, *The Glimpses of the Moon*, *The Mother's Recompense*, and *Twilight Sleep*, are not very good books. Their ostensible concerns—economic parasitism, social ostracism, Babbittry—are stale; they do not come to life in Wharton's hands. She was trying to write "her" kind of stories about women, the kind she had written with so much passion and insight during the first two decades of the twentieth century, and, although the public was happy with the new books (*Twilight Sleep* was a best-seller and *The Glimpses of the Moon* was scripted for the movies by the new young light, F. Scott Fitzgerald), the novels themselves show Edith Wharton treading water on the old issues of economics and social pressure.

In contrast, *Summer*, written during the war, and then *The Age of Innocence*, written in the immediate wake of the war, are intellectually intense books. By the time they appeared, some of what Wharton had to say was new neither in her own work nor in American fiction in general; authors such as Mary Austin, Ellen Glasgow, and David Graham Phillips were looking at many of the same problems, and arriving at their own conclusions. What quickened Wharton's argument in *Summer* and *The Age of Innocence* was the primitivism of both books, the way she saw in modern patriarchal social customs and taboos their deep prehistoric roots, and hence tenacity. The grotesque marriage forced on Charity Royall as punishment for violating the taboo against female sexual freedom and the exile inflicted on Ellen Olenska in payment for her infraction of wanting to obtain a divorce are not modern or idiosyncratic punishments. They are ancient; they are logical from a patriarchal point of view; they are symptomatic of the deeply imbedded male fear of woman that Wharton had first sketched in "The Valley of Childish Things," gone on to explore in realistic social terms in *The Fruit of the Tree*, and then in symbolic but psychohistorically revealing terms in *Ethan Frome*, and finally in prehistoric or anthropologically suggestive terms in *Summer* and *The Age of Innocence*. The war, it is safe to say, brought life to such a pitch, made fear of every sort such a known commodity, and raised to the surface (because it wiped out the surface) so many elemental facts and questions about the organization of human society that Edith Wharton was able in *Summer* and *The Age of Innocence* to bring new eyes to old themes; she was able to see deeper than ever before into the motives and values underlying the depressing patriarchal preference for the childish over the adult woman.

That being the case, the novels she wrote in the 1920s—the three mentioned, plus the last three she published: *The Children* (1928), *Hudson River Bracketed* (1929), and its sequel *The Gods Arrive* (1932)—should be her best. The issue she had felt most impelled to understand during and just after the war, the issue of the child-woman in American culture, became, with the invention of the flapper—who was known as a "jazz-baby," a "babydoll," a "cupie doll" (the labels themselves signal the figure's perfect blend of artificiality and immaturity)—the most glaring feminist issue of the decade. Edith Wharton had been thinking about the infantilization of women in America for twenty-five years and now the culture, calling the flapper new and liberated, gave forth the quintessential child-woman, one who even called her lover "daddy." Logically, Wharton should have moved smoothly from her keen analysis of May Wellandism in *The Age of Innocence* to equally penetrating studies of the contemporary flapper cult.

But careers, perhaps for the best, seldom follow the neat logic we might predict for them; and Edith Wharton, instead of lighting immediately into the flapper, took up the subject in the 1920s which was to contradict completely many of her previous arguments: motherhood. She would, as we shall see, get back to the flapper in a serious analytical way in *The Children* in 1928, a book that is one of the most perceptive novels in the twenties on the subject of America's mania for the flapper. Yet even in *The Children* Wharton's most ardent attention and concerns are reserved for her new argument about motherhood. At the very end of the decade and the beginning of the 1930s, she would raise the subject of maternity to a philosophical plane that clearly connects with her anthropological musings about patriarchy in *The Age of Innocence*; but until then her argument remained literal and specific: woman's paramount responsibility is not to herself but to her family.

The overall change in Edith Wharton's argument, which begins with *The Glimpses of the Moon* in 1922 and runs through *The Gods Arrive* ten years later, could scarcely be more drastic. Conventionally speaking, she moves from a liberal to a conservative position on the woman question. She argues that woman's duty as a mother must take precedence over her desire for personal freedom.

For Susy Lansing in *The Glimpses of the Moon*, the lesson

comes as a surprise—and to judge from the way her maternal epiphany is not prepared for throughout the novel, but appears somewhat unexpectedly at the end, it came as something of a surprise to Edith Wharton as well. She had begun the novel in 1916, and there is no hint that Susy's story will be about mothering; the first portions of the book deal with Wharton's standard pre-1920s issues: economic dependence, marriage, freedom. Susy and her husband have separated because her scheme to get married and live off the extravagant wedding gifts she knew they would receive has worked so perfectly that her husband is repelled. They have villas at their disposal, if they will as a small added tax agree to conceal their hostess's love affairs from her spouse; but Susy's husband, Nick—much like James's Densher in *The Wings of the Dove*—develops scruples once they begin benefiting from the scheme, so he bails out. Susy then finds herself alone taking care of a friend's house and small children, and to her amazement the experience makes her a new person. In these latter parts of the novel, which were written in the 1920s, her selfishness disappears in the hectic labor of caring for "the noisy argumentative Fulmers," who are for her "a school of wisdom and abnegation." Enlightened and matured, Susy gets her reward: Nick returns and, upon seeing her with an infant in her arms, thrills to "his Susy, the old Susy, and yet a new Susy, curiously transformed, transfigured almost, by the new attitude in which he beheld her . . . a thing apart, an unconditioned vision, the eternal image of the woman and the child; and in that instant everything within him was changed and renewed."[2] Wharton is serious here, and the happy couple, along with five tumbling children, whirl off on a second honeymoon.

As a problem novel, *The Glimpses of the Moon* raises a familiar Wharton question. How can an intelligent but untrained lesiure-class young woman escape economic parasitism and at the same time fulfill her desire for au-

tonomy, worthwhile occupation, and a satisfying love relationship with a man? For the first time, Wharton suggests an
answer: marriage, the home, and motherhood; and the for-
mula, recurrent throughout her subsequent novels, introduces a fundamental shift in her analysis of female human
nature and the relationship between the sexes. Wharton has
Nick Lansing at the end of *The Glimpses of the Moon* think
tenderly of another woman he almost married and then muse
over Susy's unqualified devotion to him. "It was the old contrast between the two ways of loving, the man's way and the
woman's; and after a moment it seemed to Nick natural
enough. . . . After all, there was something Providential in
such arrangements" (p. 364). This idea, normatively, becomes the premise of Edith Wharton's last novels. Man's
capacity for love is partial, and peripheral to his innermost
nature. But woman's love—steady, supportive, enduring,
total—defines her essential nature. The "Providential" aspect of this contrast, which, of course, is very old although
newly espoused by Wharton, lies in the fact that women are
meant to be mothers.

The heroine of *The Mother's Recompense* learns that fact
too late. Shortly after the turn of the century Kate Clephane
rebelled against the confinement of a loveless marriage. She
deserted her husband and infant daughter, Anne, and fled to
Europe. There, however, though "always pretending that she
felt herself free," she gradually realized "that the prison of her
marriage had been liberty" compared with the loneliness and
lack of purpose of her Riviera life.[3] So when the abandoned
daughter Anne, now grown, invites her mother to return to
New York in the early 1920s, Kate Clephane is extremely
happy.

Her renewed experience with motherhood surpasses her
expectations. "To be the background, the atmosphere, of her
daughter's life; to depend on Anne, to feel that Anne depended
on her; it was the one perfect companionship she had ever

known, the only close tie unmarred by dissimulation and distrust" (p. 87). Her new life changes Kate "from a self-centered woman, insatiable for personal excitements, into that new being, a mother, her centre of gravity in life not hers. . . . Her daughter never appeared without instantly filling up every crevice of the present, and overflowing into the past and the future, so that, even in the mother's rare lapses into despondency, life without Anne, like life before Anne, had become unthinkable" (pp. 104–5). She concludes: "Mothers oughtn't ever to leave their daughters" (p. 235). Edith Wharton agrees, and Kate Clephane pays for her desertion. By incredible coincidence the daughter falls in love with and unwittingly marries her mother's former lover, and Kate therefore exiles herself to the Riviera and her empty existence there. An old friend who loves her and shares her secret wants to marry her, but she will not permit herself the comfort. *The Mother's Recompense* thus ends in abnegation and self-punishment; and Edith Wharton clearly approves. Kate's final bereavement comprises the mother's recompense for abandoning her child and leading a promiscuous life.

The book is harsh. Kate's desertion of her baby naturally deserves censure. Moreover, we might realistically expect any reunion between such a mother and her daughter to fare badly. But the fact is that Wharton, as if intent upon torturing the mother, treats the issue unrealistically. In order to make Kate pay, not once, but twice (indeed, indefinitely), for an offense her own daughter has forgiven, the author makes the reunion perfect just to render more painful the mother's subsequent deprivation: a fate punitively contrived by means of a lover who, in a city of millions, happens to meet, fall in love with, and marry, her only child. The sad thing is that Edith Wharton likes Kate Clephane and tries to portray her situation compassionately. But the subject of mothers who refuse to mother blinds Wharton; she sacrifices Kate as a person to her theoretical preoccupation with Kate the mother.

(Theoretical because Kate's child has passed the age where she needs a lot of mothering.)

The problem, unfortunately, does not trouble Wharton's next novel for the simple reason that she makes no pretense that Pauline Manford in the satire *Twilight Sleep* is a person. She is an efficient, middle-aged, American clubwoman of the 1920s, and as such appears a "goddess of Velocity" whose life careers back and forth from weeks packed with meetings and speaking engagements to rest-cures "crammed with passive activities."[4] While her own husband longs for a sexual partner and her grown daughter has to make appointments to see her (they live in the same house), Mrs. Manford delivers inspiring public lectures on marriage and motherhood. She does once, by mistake, launch into her "Birth Control League" speech for the "National Mother's Day Association"; but this omnicompetent woman adroitly turns the faux pas to advantage (when it dawns on her what day of the week it is and therefore where she is) by attacking everything she has just finished arguing. The incident sums her up. She is able to endorse position as well as opposition on every issue because she really has no convictions; her life consists of fads.

Pauline Manford would appear merely ridiculous were it not for her failure, in Wharton's eyes, as a wife and mother. Her first husband turned alcoholic after she discarded him; their grown son is not happy; Pauline's present husband is driven half mad by the senseless rush of social activities with which his wife jams their evenings; their grown daughter, Nona, drifts. This anchorless group epitomizes Wharton's criticism of the postwar period, an era of "perpetual evasion, moral, mental, physical . . . except where money-making was concerned" (p. 56). They typify "people who regarded golf as a universal panacea . . . in a world which believed in panaceas" (p. 55). At the center of this life-by-panacea world stands Pauline Manford, advocate of painless childbirth by means of "twilight sleep" medication. And because she avoids or glosses over all pain and difficulty, she emerges as the person responsible for her family's malaise.

Wharton's criticism of Pauline may seem sound; this busy woman who is "mailed in massage and optimism" (p. 48) does neglect her family, and she does lead a foolish, frenetically pointless life. Still, Wharton weights the case unfairly and wages her attack sloppily. Pauline's lapses in taste attract as much criticism as her lapses in principle or good judgment; and, snobbishness aside, Wharton fails to make Pauline a fully dimensioned character (even Undine Spragg has more depth) and then proceeds to ridicule her shallowness, conformity, and, above all, the fatuity of her pseudo-professional life. The last failing betrays the basic flaw in the book's social criticism. The career Pauline manufactures is ludicrous; but that does not make the author's implicit alternative—model mother and homemaker—any less ridiculous for a woman with grown children.

In Edith Wharton's novels about the American 1920s there is a remarkable change in attitude toward women and marriage. Whereas she formerly sympathized with aspirant women trapped by marriage and the lack of desirable alternatives, she now argues that marriage and domestic life are woman's best means of self-fulfillment. For Susy Branch in *The Glimpses of the Moon* the idea works. She and her husband love each other and share a conversion in values. However, the same thesis proclaimed punitively in *The Mother's Recompense* and simplistically in *Twilight Sleep* lacks persuasion: Kate Clephane and Pauline Manford have passed the child-rearing age. If it begins to seem that Wharton really recommends motherhood less for women's happiness than for children's welfare and the culture's stability, *The Children*, Wharton's next novel about the period, confirms the suspicion. Yet in its indictment of negligent flapper-mothers, *The Children* argues a legitimate case. Young children do need mothers. For their sake, part of adult life for many women may require sacrifice and the temporary sublimation of personal goals.

Mothering, of course, was not new as a topic in Wharton's fiction. After focusing on the subject in *Sanctuary*, at the outset of her career in 1903, she moved it to the background in her next six books; she used maternity to help the reader understand and judge important women characters. Undine's neglect of her son and her attempt to barter him for annulment money emphasize her ruthless selfishness in *The Custom of the Country*. In *The Age of Innocence* May's estrangement from her children, who feel they must shelter her from life, underscores her arrested development. Similarly, Bessy's manic behavior toward her daughter in *The Fruit of the Tree* highlights her unhappiness and immaturity: she either overwhelms the child with affection or forgets her existence entirely.

On the other hand, the admirable women in Wharton's earlier novels make or would make good mothers. Justine ably supervises her adopted daughter's upbringing in *The Fruit of the Tree* and cherishes the affection she and Cicely develop for one another. (Analogously, Sophy's success as a governess in *The Reef* displays her intelligence and good nature.) Anna Leath—Wharton's most sensitive mother— encourages in Effie the independence and expressiveness her own upbringing repressed; and the value she places on serving as a worthy model for her little girl in *The Reef* shows how she prizes her daughter's respect. Charity, pregnant but unmarried, recoils from abortion in *Summer* because she wants to mother her child. And, though poignant because so naive, her fantasy about working as a prostitute to support the infant in luxury accentuates the generosity and tenderness she hides from the puritanical populace of North Dormer. Finally, Lily Bart's warm response to an acquaintance's baby at the end of *The House of Mirth* distinguishes her from the coldhearted pleasure-seekers of the leisure class. Thus maternal dispositions in the earlier novels serve repeatedly as one significant measure of character; with the exception of Ellen Olenska in *The Age of Innocence*, each woman's behavior or potential as a mother helps define her. The contrast is that motherhood gains central importance in Wharton's later novels, and the switch in emphasis and outlook creates major difficulties. It commits her to depicting children, for which she had no gift. It requires that she describe in some detail the experience of motherhood, about which she knew little. It permits her to ignore male characters even more than usual. It leads her to idealize feminine self-sacrifice (a sentimental notion she had sagely moved away from very early in her career). All combine to undermine the quality of her last novels because all make demands that call up the worst rather than the best of Edith Wharton as a writer.

Critics have wondered about the decline in quality of these later novels, speculating that either Wharton's advanced age during the 1920s or her distance from her subject, America, or the serializing of her novels in popular magazines that catered to women might account for the deterioration. Although each of these factors contributes, it should not be forgotten that Wharton was in her seventies when she wrote her unfinished last novel *The Buccaneers* (published posthumously in 1938), yet many readers consider it one of her finest. Nor should it be ignored that, although her life abroad following the war did cut her off from the American scene, she set more than half of the action of her postwar novels in Europe, the arena she then knew best. Still these novels do not compare favorably with her earlier ones set on either side of the Atlantic. Also, Wharton had serialized many of her books before and reflected popular feminine interests in them without compromising quality; and even if she did consciously relax her standards to please the readership of magazines such as *The Delineator* and *The Pictorial Review* (hard as that is to imagine, given her lifelong assault on mediocrity of every sort), the earnestness of her last novels argues that, audience aside, Edith Wharton was writing out of conviction. As if to enforce the point, she listed three of them, *The Children*, *Hudson River Bracketed*, and *The Gods Arrive*, among the five favorite she had written (the other two being *Summer* and *The Custom of the Country*).[5] Age, expatriation, and commercialism may explain part of what went wrong, relatively speaking, with Wharton's fiction about the twenties; but certainly another important factor, and one that has been overlooked so far, is the author's near obsession with the subject of motherhood, which, in her hands, results in the problems already mentioned.

Why, then, the intense interest on Wharton's part? No single fact can explain her new fascination with motherhood or fully account for her switch in argument. For one thing, she more than likely had personal reasons for becoming sentimental about mothering in her sixties. She had no children of her own, and many of her oldest friends were dead or getting close to death. James had died in 1916; Mary Cadwalader Jones was an old woman by now; Walter Berry was getting old and would not live through the twenties; several of Wharton's servants with whom she had lived all her adult life had already died or entered last illnesses. Clearly despite all her wealth and success, she was feeling a new and especially difficult type of loneliness; it is very probable that there were times when she wished she had a child to think about or talk with. (Probably it is not coincidental that the irresponsible mothers she is hardest on in her fiction, Kate Clephane and Pauline Manford, are mothers of grown children, as Wharton's would be at this time in her life had she had any.) During the war she grew quite solicitous of two young soldiers the age of sons or grandsons, Ronald Simmons and her second cousin "Bo" Rhinelander, who both were killed. Philomène de la Forest-Divonne, too young to stand in anything but a filial position of the great author, visited Edith Wharton at her home north of Paris, the Pavillon Colombe, in the mid-1930s and left this rare glimpse into Wharton's possible regrets:

> Then, into the salon where the fire gleamed equally with the last roses, Edith brought the past. She brought it in the form of an album where there were carefully pasted (amid a number of rare photographs) clippings of critical articles about her first writings. I would sacrifice several visits, a trip, many walks with her than have this day lost to me! . . . It is one of my precious memories; on that afternoon I felt what Edith *could have been for the children she never had.* . . .
> With how much delicious affection she made me a participant in her earliest memories. And how certain I was that day (I have remained so ever since) of all the warmth hidden beneath the snow.[6]

That Wharton herself felt a daughter in particular might have brought her great pleasure in her old age is evident in two of her best shorter pieces written during the 1920s, the novella *The Old Maid* and the short story, "Roman Fever." Both are about women, like Wharton at the time, of an age to have grown daughters; and the theme of each, as she expresses it in *The Old Maid*, is "maternal passion," the fierce emotional attachment of a woman to her child. Significantly this passion in each story is felt only toward an extraordinary daughter— one who is vibrant and daring—and in both cases this young woman is the offspring of an illicit affair her mother had as a young woman. How much Edith Wharton as an older woman may have longed, at least at times, for such a daughter is only barely concealed in the two fictions.

Small children, on the other hand, according to her friend Margaret Chanler, unnerved Wharton. "I have seen her," Chanler says, "really frightened in the presence of children." She goes on, and the comment certainly describes the strained portrait of mothering in *The Glimpses of the Moon*: "With all her great intelligence she knew nothing of the natural pleasure our children give us: she interpreted maternal devotion as heroic self-sacrifice—indeed she seemed to look on all family life as more or less of a calamity."[7] Yet Wharton at one point took six orphans into her home during the war, and their bubbliness seems to have been her inspiration for the fond portraits of little children that she tried, without much success, to bring to life in both *The Glimpses of the Moon* and *The Children*. (Her affection for Royall and Elisina Tyler's little boy also suggests delight in small children.) The important thing, however, whatever Wharton's personal comfort or discomfort with young children, is that for the first time she became very interested in their welfare and in the conduct of their mothers in the 1920s. Probably this had something to do with her own age and childlessness; surely it had a lot to do with the war she had recently been through and the new world she now saw around her. Both drove her to think about motherhood.

The First World War, as was the case with many people directly involved with it, had a delayed but permanent and profound effect on Edith Wharton. Biography rightly lauds her stupendous contribution to the war effort and the honors that accrued because of it. Less documented because harder—if not impossible—to document is the emotional effect the war clearly had. Unlike most Americans, especially women, Edith Wharton not only witnessed the war firsthand, but also as it threatened her adopted homeland, France. Moreover, in contrast to American soldiers, or paramilitary writers seeking adventure and heroic material, she experienced the war as an older person and a civilian. She did visit the front, but most of the time she labored at supportive tasks in and around Paris. She traveled through provincial areas destroyed by the German army and feared that fate for Paris, the center of civilization in her opinion. Month after month she pleaded for American reinforcement and money, while refugees, many of them starving women and children, depended on her to find them shelter and food. Meanwhile, in overcrowded hospitals young men less than half her age died, or struggled to recuperate from injuries that left them, in her own words, "hardly men any longer . . . merely vivisected animals, without eyes, without faces."[8]

It is common to read of a war's effect on the thinking and art of a man who has been close to it—of a Whitman or a Crane or a Hemingway. We have even learned to romanticize their experiences. Less commonly do we reflect on war's reality for women. Yet Edith Wharton perceived and experienced life during the war as she never had before, and the shock was never fully to leave her. Shelter, food, physical courage, emotional stamina, protection of the young and the helpless— these comprised the daily business of life for four years, and pain and suffering the daily facts. The sustained threat of annihilation—of human beings and of civilization itself— convinced her that the preservation of cultural continuity and the nurture of the young must take precedence over all individual ambitions, those of women included. She had seen too many homes and beloved pieces of architecture destroyed and too many children and young men mutilated in body or spirit or both, or killed outright, to believe ever again that anything could be more important than the responsibility to support life, particularly the life of children and the life of art, which is preserved in the culture we inherit.

At the very beginning of the war Wharton said "*My* sense is completely of living again in the year 1000, with the last trump imminent."[9] Her worst fear—that the Germans would win—was not realized. But her statement is important nonetheless because it speaks of life being reduced to primitive realities. It articulates her fear that civilization was being forced backward, into the dark. Others, of course, shared that vision of time turning back to some barbarous point in the uncivilized past. Margaret Deland, writing of the war in *Small Things* in 1919, worried about emotions "slipping into the

primitive"—so visceral and violent was the hatred for the
Germans (which she shared but tried to modulate).[10]
Another writer completely different from either Wharton or
Deland, Jane Addams, described in 1916 "desolated women,
stripped by war of all their warm domestic interests and of
children long cherished in affectionate solicitude. . . . Forced
to look into the black depths of primitive human nature,
occasionally one of these broken-hearted women would ignore the strident claims of the present and would insist that
the war was cutting at the very taproots of the basic human
relations so vitally necessary to the survival of civilization."[11]
Although more sophisticated probably than the women Addams had in mind, Wharton nevertheless knew their fear.

Her novels about the postwar period consistently emphasize the seriousness of life and the disastrous consequences
of trying to evade pain and suffering and responsibility. After
several years of outspoken anger, Wharton was full of pride
and patriotism when America finally entered the war. But
after the war, when the United States withdrew into international isolationism, she was plunged once again into horror at
her compatriots' apathy and stupidity. Her friend Sara Norton
expressed disgust over the isolationist policy, and Wharton
replied, "I say nothing about what you say of public affairs
except that I agree with you on every point, and am humiliated to the soul at being what is now known as an 'American.' All that I thought American in a true sense is gone, and I
see nothing but vain-glory, crassness, and total ignorance—which of course is the core of the whole evil."[12] She
looked at the American Roaring Twenties and saw a youth
cult that reduced the world to a kindergarten: a chaotic play-
ground where life was turned into a game, carefree and
hedonistic. But human life, she protested, was not a game.
The war had taught her, if it had taught her nothing else, that
like all of creation human life emanates from something deep
and mysterious and is therefore painful as well as joyful;

corporate as well as individual; care-full as well as carefree.
America's infatuation with the flapper, the national glibness
about divorce, the neglect of children, the self-absorbed quest
for thrills and instant happiness, the mania for change for its
own sake, the scorn for intellectual independence or disciplined art: all evidenced a retreat from adult responsibility
and the difficult realities of mature human experience that the
war had impressed on Edith Wharton. The focus of her social
criticism had to shift in the 1920s. The cultural problem her
later novels attack is not really that women lack freedom—
though ostensibly that remains a theme—but that most of
them, along with the rest of society, have been liberated into a
world of meaningless, childish activity which has lost touch
with the first principle of existence, what she would come in
her last two novels to call "The Mothers."

The shift is apparent in *The Glimpses of the Moon*, *The
Mother's Recompense*, and *Twilight Sleep* but not yet very
interesting because Wharton's thinking in these books is, for
her, not sophisticated. The first two novels are melodramas
(soap operas actually) and the last reads almost like a poor
imitation of Sinclair Lewis. With its diffuse plotting, caricatures, and gimmicky capitalizations, *Twilight Sleep* might
well be dedicated to *Babbitt*: it is as if the mentor becomes the
pupil's imitator and, twice removed, parodies herself. Not
until *The Children*, in 1928, was Wharton able to do justice,
intellectually, to her postwar argument about mothers and
flappers.

The book's title, *The Children*, refers to seven Wheater
children who are neglected yet fought over by their various
and repeatedly divorced parents, who are fashionable jazzy
people too preoccupied with themselves to worry about children. Middle-aged Martin Boyne, the novel's main character,
meets these children on an Atlantic steamer en route to the
Riviera; he is going to visit the woman he has always loved,
Rose Sellars, a recently widowed woman close to his own

age. But he falls in love with fifteen-year-old Judith Wheater, the oldest of the seven children, consequently lets Rose break their engagement, and then proposes to the girl. She thinks he is joking. Martin Boyne, still a bachelor when the book ends, has given up Rose Sellars for Judith Wheater, a girl so young that she can love him only as a paternal figure.

Although *The Children* intertwines many Wharton concerns and themes, some old and some new, what it does finally and most successfully is explain the impossibility of having "grown-up" women, women whose talents might include being good mothers, in a culture that worships little-girl-women, flappers. Judith Wheater's mother, Joyce, is a perfect flapper and a perfectly horrendous mother, as Martin Boyne is well aware. What he does not see is the parallel between his own "love" for her daughter Judith, who naturally thinks of him as a father, and the culture's adoration of babydoll women. He finds his own preference for Judith over Rose Sellars surprising but not abnormal, at the same time that he abjures his countrymen's preference for the flapper (an artificial version of Judith) over the New Woman ideal she has replaced. But Edith Wharton, of course, sees the parallel between Boyne's infatuation with Judith and America's with the flapper, who is ironically the heiress of demure May Welland; and she also sees that it is precisely Boyne's type of fear of the mature sexuality of Rose Sellars that inspires the whole patriarchal complex, personal and national.

Wharton pairs Rose and Judith as she had many heroines in the past: Justine and Bessy in *The Fruit of the Tree*, Mattie and Zeena in *Ethan Frome*, Anna and Sophy in *The Reef*, Ellen and May in *The Age of Innocence*. Her purpose in *The Children* (she never used the device of the dual heroine twice for exactly the same purpose) is to give us Martin Boyne's basic point of view on woman. Therefore Wharton gives Rose and Judith much in common. Each likes children; each in her own way loves Boyne; each has a quality of being "different" from the "standardized" beauty of other women or girls in the 1920s.[13] And although Rose declares that Judith is young enough to be her daughter, the two look like sisters with their brown hair and dark eyes; moreover both are slim, agile, and buoyant. It is true that Rose, who is twice Judith's age, is more educated and sophisticated; and, as a widow, she is sexually experienced. But these differences, the result of age and circumstance, are not as fundamental as the similarities between the characters which point on a symbolic level to the idea that Rose Sellars, the woman Boyne rejects, represents Judith Wheater grown-up. Figuratively, that is, Boyne does not choose between two women but between two stages of development in woman, as he perceives her: the child and the grown-up.

What he decides, after meeting Judith, is that Rose is too adaptable yet too independent; too worldly yet too inexperienced; too meddling yet too aloof; too complicated yet too simple. Obviously Boyne needs to find fault with Rose Sellars, who of course has her shortcomings but is on the whole an extremely attractive person. The fact is, Boyne does not want a grown-up woman, and it is Rose's sexual availability that especially alienates him. When he could not have her, his ardor was acute. "Now there was no resistance—and his passion lay with folded wings" (p. 85; cf. 40). In his beloved, Martin Boyne wants a sexually unattainable, and only partially formed, dependent person who excites his imagination and needs his protection. Rose Sellars does not meet those requirements.

Fifteen-year-old Judith Wheater, however, does. Although she is simply an attractive adolescent, burdened but competent beyond her years because of the parental responsibility she has had to assume in default of her own parents, in Boyne's eyes she appears "an imponderable and elusive creature," "a young Daphne, half emerging into reality, half caught in the foliage of fairyland" (pp. 36–37, 265). He tries to organize his impression of her:

Whatever she was, she was only intermittently, as if her body were the mere vehicle of her moods . . . with hardly any material identity of its own. . . . "A strange little creature who changes every hour, hardly seems to have any personality of her own except when she's mothering her flock. Then she's extraordinary: playmate, mother and governess all in one; and the best of each in its way. As for her very self, when she's not with them, you grope for her identity and find an instrument the wind plays on, a looking-glass that reflects the clouds, a queer little sensitive plate, very little and very sensitive." (pp. 36–37)

Adolescent Judith Wheater, unlike May in *The Age of Innocence* or Bessy in *The Fruit of the Tree*, is a natural and complicated mixture of immaturity and maturity, and as such very human. Nevertheless, Boyne sees only a selfless sprite: vivacious yet docile and maternal yet innocent. If his idealized image of the girl bears remarkable resemblance to the romanticized May of Archer's imagination at the end of *The Age of Innocence* and the etherealized Bessy of Amherst's delusion at the end of *The Fruit of the Tree,* it is no accident. In all three cases the man's image of the child-woman significantly distorts the female human nature it supposedly reflects, and the parallel invites generalization. Wharton suggests that the mythicized image of the American child-woman, whether cherished in the mind of one man or of the culture at large, mirrors nature very imperfectly because it originates less in nature than in the masculine imagination, which perceives woman from the point of view of its own desires and fears, rather than her objective reality. In a broad sense, this masculine impulse has appeared in almost all of Wharton's men—in Lawrence Selden, George Darrow, Ralph Marvell, Ethan Frome, and Mr. Royall as well as in Boyne, Amherst, and Archer. Each manifests the same tendency to perceive a woman not as she is but as he would have her. Indeed, what is the Pygmalion impulse, so ubiquitous in Wharton's novels, but the wish to project a preconceived, or mythicized, image of woman onto a real human being?[14]

Specifically, the idealized Judith of Boyne's mind's eye grows out of his desire, as Wharton's use of the name *Boy*ne makes perhaps too clear, to *be* one of "The Children," and that fear in turn grows out of his fear of Rose's sexuality. Not that sexual relations with a woman in and of themselves frighten Boyne. Like most of Wharton's heroes, "in the course of his life . . . much easy love had come his way" (p. 84). But Boyne, again like most of Wharton's men, fears the intimacy of a sustained, adult, heterosexual relationship based on intellectual, moral, and emotional as well as physical reciprocity. He prefers the "boyish excitement" (p. 243), the "half-fatherly attitude" (p. 245), "the frank elder-brotherly affection" (p. 247) he can exhibit in the nursery with the Wheater children. "He and they understood each other. . . . 'The fact is, we're none of us grown up,' he reflected, hugging himself for being on the children's side of the eternal barrier" (p. 247).

Martin Boyne's happiness in the nursery explains his attraction to Judith. In the children's world Judith loves him with unquestioning devotion, does not call upon him to cope with adult sexuality, and never challenges his authority. In effect, as an adopted member of the Wheater brood, mothered by a female whose sexual appeal he cannot admit, Boyne recaptures the infantile identity of omnipotent yet protected child—with one crucial improvement. In this utopian nursery, woman is a nurturer whose frightening power in the actual experience of infancy can be denied because, here, she is just another child. Clearly, Boyne's love for the girl indicates fear of woman's power and concomitant desire to retreat into an artificial pregenital world of maternal love, minus maternal power. He prefers Judith to Rose because his relationship with the "little-girl-mother" (p. 38)—whether as father and daughter, or elder brother and little sister, or omnipotent child and gratifying mother—weighs in favor of his power and therefore never threatens him. In no way, he repeatedly reassures himself, despite Judith's obvious sexual appeal (which Rose but not Boyne is able to recognize), are they man and woman.

Boyne epitomizes the American male's fear of woman, his erotic immaturity, which, as Leslie Fiedler has pointed out in *Love and Death in the American Novel*, the nation's literature so often dramatizes. As Fiedler puts it: "Is there not, our writers ask over and over, a sentimental relationship at once erotic and immaculate, a union which commits its participants neither to society nor sin—and yet one which is able to symbolize the union of the ego with the id, the thinking self with its rejected impulses?"[15] In Boyne, Edith Wharton, who is never mentioned by Fiedler, raises that question and answers: no. Furthermore, in her view the erotic immaturity of American men as a group deserves less sympathy than criticism; for, although pathologically understandable, it serves nonetheless to rationalize patriarchal attitudes that oppress women. As the literary critic Katharine M. Rogers observes (the remark, though not made about Martin Boyne in *The Children*, might as well be): "If the male members of a patriarchal society were altogether confident about their superior power and capacity, they would feel no anxiety about their status and—on this ground at least—no hostility to women. But of course they cannot; the patriarch always has the haunting memory of his original dependence on his mother. Hence he must keep reassuring himself that woman is really weak and insignificant."[16]

Though Wharton regrets Boyne's rejection of Rose Sellars, she does not criticize his love for Judith Wheater. His preference for her is simply rather sad. (Were he to persuade her to marry him, which he tries but fails to do, moral judgments no doubt would appear.) Wharton can and does, however, criticize the cultural disorder that results from such male American fear of and consequent flight from adult heterosexual relationships.

When Rose Sellars, writing in response to Boyne's description of Judith at the beginning of the book, happens on the label "little-girl-mother (sounds almost as nauseating as 'child-wife,' doesn't it?)" she says, and jokingly adds "luckily you'll be parting soon, or I should expect to see you arrive here with the girl-bride of the movies" (p. 38), Wharton—by having the novel's one admirable adult juxtapose the terms "little-girl-mother," "child-wife," and "girl-bride"—underscores the overriding social criticism of *The Children*. Because Boyne loathes the flapper as a perversion of womanhood, he never realizes that his own attraction to Judith mimics the culture's adoration of the grossly artificial child-woman of the 1920s, the flapper. But it does, of course. Just as his love for Judith suggests one man's yearning to escape to an exciting but nonthreatening nursery-world, so the American idolatry of the flapper—a human baby-doll— indicates a whole culture's flight from adulthood. To make the point absolutely clear, Wharton portrays in *The Children* three flappers: each, figuratively speaking, a child-wife and a little-girl-mother and one, in addition, a movie queen.

Flappers appear in other Wharton novels set in the 1920s—Lilla Gates in *The Mother's Recompense* and Lita Wyant in *Twilight Sleep*—and the author obviously dislikes both. She makes them ignorant, selfish, trivial, promiscuous, careless, and, above all, childish. For despite her semblance of autonomy, the flapper as Wharton presents her only superficially defies the old ideal of docile femininity. Pleasing men remains her object in life; she is not really independent or self-determining. She daringly apes those conditions to make herself all the more exciting a conquest, all the more valuable an acquisition. In actuality, however, she lives in as perennial a state of unnatural childishness as carmine lips of the same glossy texture, and blue-grey eyes with long lashes that curved backward (like the bust's) as though they were painted on her lids" (p. 48). (In an earlier version of the passage Wharton had actually used for "wooden bust" and "bust's" the terms "wooden dolls" and "doll's" before revising to make the doll symbolism a little more subtle.[17]) Asked his opinion of the similarly middle-aged Syb Lullmer, who looks as if "she might be Judy's age" and "is always chock full of drugs" to keep her calm but vivacious, Boyne simply says "I think she's hideous" (p. 153). These three women are hideous. They appear as caricatures because they have made of themselves caricatures: painted-doll imitations of girls.

Wharton permits no sympathy for these characters because, unlike the child-women May Welland and Bessy Westmore, the arrested women in *The Children* demean themselves. Worse yet, as mothers who refuse to provide the love and guidance their children need, their complicity in their own infantilization is not merely disgusting, but immoral. There is nothing charming about Joyce Wheater's gay remark: "Why Judy's like a mother to me, I assure you. . . . She loves it, you know! It's her hobby" (p. 54). Presumably, Syb Lullmer's daughter, the same age as Judith and significantly named Doll, had the same hobby thrust on her, until she committed suicide at the age of fourteen. The spectacle of adults willingly turning themselves into children, while their own children go motherless, appalls Edith Wharton.

Although her repeated attacks on the flapper grow redundant and her ferocity on the subject begins to grate at times, Wharton's abhorrence of the postwar child-woman reflects genuine dismay for a culture that has lost its mind and soul—as *The Children* avers, a culture grown "clockless and conscienceless" (p. 81). Women at last had some choice about their lives and identity, and the flapper—socially pressured of course, but not coerced—symbolizes the depressing motherhood. Lita Wyant and Joyce Wheater and Syb Lullmer illustrate the type of mother the flapper makes.

The Children is Wharton's best book about the Roaring Twenties. Old-fashioned Martin Boyne despises the flapper; yet in her attempt to dematerialize herself into something imponderable and elusive and translucent she responds, on the cultural level, to the same masculine yearning to escape adult life that motivates Boyne's attraction to the imponderable, elusive Judith Wheater of his imagination. Indeed, the thematic unity of the novel stems from the ironic parallel between his romanticization of Judith on the one hand, and, on the other, American idolatry of the flapper. Male fear of adult women may be poignant on the individual level of Boyne's confused love for the literal child-woman, Judith, whom he idealizes. It is abominable, however, turned into a national cult in which baby-doll sex-queens become idols and traditional human virtues such as integrity and responsibility and self-knowledge have no importance. Edith Wharton sums up her despair over postwar American culture in the title of *The Children,* which describes every character in the book but one: the lonely "grown-up" woman, Rose Sellars, who is childless.

The Age of Innocence, in 1920, marked the end of Edith Wharton's Progressive Era argument with America, a phase largely political and economic in its analyses and assumptions. The position of women in American society—past or present, elevated or low on the scale of class—Wharton, like many of her peers, viewed as the consequence of determinable human laws and systems. Woman was where she was because patriarchal custom had placed her there, and it therefore followed that to understand the laws and assumptions of the patriarchate was to understand fully, completely, the reality of woman's situation. Such analysis might not lead to any change in that situation. Indeed much of Wharton's purpose in undertaking rigorous analysis seems to have been to demonstrate how difficult, perhaps impossible, change would be. Many people in the first two decades of the twentieth century believed that progress had arrived: it was argued that woman was emancipated and only a few hangovers from the past remained, and they would not linger long. Edith Wharton was never among the optimists. She was cautious, probing, skeptical; the New Woman was not yet a reality in her opinion and, given patriarchal attitudes, might never be. In this dissent, historically speaking, Edith Wharton was absolutely right. Still, she was of her generation in approaching the woman question as a completely rational one, one that was a matter of finding the correct logical questions to ask—political, economic, psychological—and then equally logical answers, depending on whether one was looking for solutions or causes, would be forthcoming. For all her pessimism, the core impulse of her early work, her repeated attacks on the limitations inflicted on women, betrays a deeply guarded, a privately leashed and hidden hopefulness. No one, except a mad person, attacks the immutable.

Then came the war. It changed the world on Edith Wharton and consequently her way of responding to it. She tried to write her cool, analytical novels and instead wrote highly emotional ones. She was sickened by the flapper; she was obsessed by the subject of bad and good mothering. The failure of American culture before the First World War, she had argued in every book about the prewar era, lay in its immoral and wasteful oppression of women. From Lily Bart to Ellen Olenska, her heroines testify to America's shameful refusal to extend to female members of society its dream of freedom and the opportunity for self-direction. Few writers can match the insight and controlled passion Edith Wharton brought to that issue. Beyond question, her prewar belief in the individual's right to freedom and her criticism of institutionalized injustice place her in the first ranks of classic American literature. But the war recast the world. The terrible experience of the event itself, exacerbated by Jazz-Age America's suppression of that sobering turn of affairs, permanently redefined the cultural problem for Wharton. As she saw it civilization had nearly been obliterated and the world had to regain stability. This mission of saving civilization she assigned to women. (Men, it seems, were utterly out of the question: even Lawrence Selden and George Darrow seem attractive human beings next to insecure boys like Nick Lansing in *The Glimpses of the Moon* and Martin Boyne in *The Children* or Vance Weston in *Hudson Bracketed* and *The Gods Arrive,* and those three are the best of the postwar lot.) In Wharton's opinion, the perpetuation of human culture and of life itself—the nurture of artists and children—demanded that women, recklessly self-absorbed at precisely the time in history when personal sacrifice was imperative, devote themselves to mothering in the interest of establishing anew cultural continuity.

Of course this endorsement of motherhood thoroughly contradicts Edith Wharton's earlier argument with America, her contention that women were not but should be free. The new argument is fundamentally emotional and conservative and says that women must sublimate their desires for freedom to the higher duty of serving their families and the culture as mothers. Susy Lansing does that in *The Glimpses of the Moon* and is happy for it, as will also be the case with Halo Tarrant in *The Gods Arrive.* Kate Clephane does not do it in *The Mother's Recompense* and is unhappy for it, as are Pauline Manford in *Twilight Sleep* (her daughter gets shot) and Joyce Wheater in *The Children* (her infant dies). As a realistic, literal argument Wharton's endorsement of motherhood is simplistic and reactionary, and in major ways it is responsible for the deterioration in quality of her novels about the twenties; their preachiness, their disposition toward caricature, their sentimentality and vindictiveness, their bathos, their unabashed misandry.

It is to be regretted that she became so focused on mothering—not because mothers cannot be interesting characters or mothering a worthy subject (indeed, at a time when Hemingway, Fitzgerald, and Sinclair Lewis were villifying mothers, respect for motherhood was sorely needed) but because Edith Wharton was not the author to make mothers and their lives credible and important and at the same time human. She had never resolved her feelings toward her own mother, toward whom she harbored a blighting, disproportionate anger that often comes out in her portraits of less-than-perfect mothers in the fiction, and she had no substantial personal experience with raising children to help her develop compassion and respect for mothers as people rather than roles. Ironically, although Wharton differs in avowing genuine interest in mothers, she fails in her treatment of motherhood for much the same reason that the younger, male authors of the 1920s failed. She intellectualizes motherhood and manipulates maternal characters to argue a thesis about American culture: her mothers function as marionettes rather than as fully dimensioned, complicated, female human beings.

Additionally, her preoccupation with the subject of mothering narrowed and foreshortened her social criticism, which had previously distinguished itself by the way it could see around and beyond the obvious. Although popular opinion even now often regards the twenties as a period of significant liberation for women, historians rightly point out that the postwar decade did not build on the progress that was made before the war and in many ways women actually lost ground despite the passage of the Nineteenth Amendment (some would say because of it). A real need existed during the 1920s for continued and profound change in woman's image and women's lives. The work of the Progressive Era's Woman Movement was not over—the optimism Edith Wharton had argued with for twenty years *had* been premature. If the war had not intervened, making the conservation of culture and life itself more important to Wharton than the rights of women to live autonomous lives, it might have been Edith Wharton, one is tempted to say, who could have written novels about women in the 1920s to hold their own against the fearful or downright hostile fictions of the period. Her attacks on the flapper suggest as much. She, unlike many writers of the day, saw that the flapper was not liberated, not attractive, and certainly not powerful, as some of her younger male colleagues would have their readers believe. The flapper was just another human doll, another little-girl-woman. But the subject of mothering trapped Wharton into replacing one severely limited image—the flapper—with another: the self-less mother; and her fiction about the 1920s, as a consequence, is neither intellectually nor artistically up to the standard of her books about the problems and failed promise of Progressive America.

The Mothers

The last turn in Edith Wharton's argument may be the most surprising. The spirit of the Progressive Era with its secular faith in hard analytical reason was far behind her by the end of the 1920s. She was getting old now; she had lived through the most devastating war the world had yet known and then lived to see her native land giddily, childishly, try to dance and party the memory away; she was thinking about death and deathlessness and the springs of life from which art rises. Never before a religious person, at this time in her life she began to show signs of developing some sort of religious faith, or what might more accurately be called a sympathy with faith itself—an inclination toward the spiritual and mystical as sources of truth and healing. She mused to Elisina Tyler very late in her life: "Religious thought is certainly a great power. The greatest of all. It embraces everything."[1] As the title of her last novel, *The Gods Arrive*, announces almost with relief, a new and healing vision, one fundamentally religious rather than political, had begun to germinate for Edith Wharton.

She finished *The Children* early in 1928 and immediately set to work on *Hudson River Bracketed*, which she published in 1929, and then its sequel, *The Gods Arrive*, which came out in 1932. At her death in 1937 she had another book well under way, *The Buccaneers*, a historical romance, but it remained for her literary executor to complete the manuscript (using Wharton's outline) and bring the book out in 1938. The last novels she actually brought to conclusion and saw through publication were *Hudson River Bracketed* and *The Gods Arrive*.

Together, they summarize her criticism of postwar American values and attempt to synthesize her new endorsement of motherhood with her lifelong belief in woman's right to self-determination. The synthesis is not very successful: it is achieved at the cost of the heroine's integrity as a believable character. But on the figurative level, Wharton's final argument is fascinating. She moves beyond the subject of literal motherhood to meditation on the maternal principle itself and, combining literary, anthropological, and religious ideas, evokes the gods in which she believes the modern world stands in need. Those gods are female. They are the Mothers to whom Goethe had his Faust descend; they are the primordial maternal center of life whose loss to the Western world is recorded in Aeschylus's *Oresteia*, from which Edith Wharton at an early age took the image of the Furies that was to stay with her throughout her imaginative life but only in old age acquire the power of gender. They are—the Mothers of Wharton's last finished work, which she needed two volumes to contain—her mystical solution to a lifetime of tough-minded analysis, argument and debate on the subject of woman.

That the first principle might be female rather than male was by the early 1930s a familiar idea. Faulkner uses it in *Light in August*, published in 1932, the same year as Wharton's *The Gods Arrive*. Before him in the mid-twenties Hemingway had invested in Brett Ashley in *The Sun Also Rises* an awesome sexual power which, symbolically, likewise calls up myths of the Great Goddess, with her power over life and death, fertility and sterility. And before either Faulkner or Hemingway, Willa Cather in *My Ántonia* (1918) and *O Pioneers!* (1913) had imagined female characters whose strength clearly attaches them to some mystic realm of earthy mother-goddesses. So when Edith Wharton directed her thoughts on motherhood and cultural continuity (or renewal) toward the mythic, toward the concept of the Great Mother of prehistory, she was moving into modern but not uncharted or untrod territory. Other writers were simultaneously engaged in the intellectual adventure that anthropologists and a few imaginative classicists had, before them, begun to explore.

Nor is Wharton's arrival at the Mothers without preface in her own work. Its first glimmer should be traced to the elemental fear of woman that *Ethan Frome*, in fairy-tale guise in 1911, dramatized; and if the mythic and anthropological arguments and motifs after *Ethan Frome* are taken as a whole, and taken seriously, it could certainly be said that Wharton, like Cather, anticipated rather than joined the moderns of the 1920s—Joyce, T. S. Eliot, Hemingway, Faulkner—in their use of ancient myths to plumb contemporary depths (and shallows). The erotic power of Undine Spragg, Wharton's "warrior Queen" in *The Custom of the Country* (1913), the violation of the incest taboo in *Summer* (1918), the tribal sexual politic of patriarchal old New York in *The Age of Innocence* (1920): these, along with the primitive terror of the female in the story about Ethan Frome, suggest how early Wharton's interest in the prehistoric was taking shape.

Hudson River Bracketed and *The Gods Arrive* take that interest in the prehistoric further than any of Wharton's preceding work, although literally the books merely tell the story of one young man's maturation. In the first novel, Vance Weston, a fledgling writer, marries a sweet child-woman, Laura Lou, but then finds himself falling in love with Halo Tarrant, an intelligent young woman marooned in a stupid marriage. Laura Lou dies at the end of the first novel, and *The Gods Arrive* opens with Vance and Halo, who has left her husband, living together in Europe. Vance tires of Halo, whose honesty about his work he solicits but then finds threatening, and decides to marry his first love, Floss Delaney, a glamorous "vamp" in the tradition of Undine Spragg.

Surprisingly Floss is the prime agent of Vance's transformation. She jilts him and he returns to Halo, who is now pregnant with their child, and the two begin a new life in America that will be rooted in intellectual comradeship, marriage, and parenthood. Both books are transparently didactic, and their purpose, stated very simply, is to disillusion Vance so that he can receive the regenerative truth forecast by the title of the second novel, which Wharton took from the conclusion of Emerson's poem "Give All to Love": "Heartily know, / When half-gods go, / The gods arrive." The gods who arrive for Vance are the Mothers.

Wharton took the image of the Mothers from Goethe and then developed it into her own mystical philosophy of maternal wisdom, which she applies in her last two novels both to the marital bond and to the artist's creative process. In his honest moments Vance scorns the verbal acrobatics of his fashionable literary friends; he "felt the hollowness underfoot, and said to himself: 'No, life's not like that, people are not like that. The real stuff is way down, not on the surface.' When he got hold of *Faust* at the Willows [the old house Halo inherits and restores], and came to the part about the mysterious Mothers, moving in subterranean depths among the primal forms of life, he shouted out: 'That's it—the fellows who write those books are all Motherless!' "[2] Wharton has Vance Weston remain similarly Motherless, blithe and shallow, until he is initiated into the Mothers' wisdom by his maternal grandmother, a wise earthy old lady named Mrs. Scrimser.

As Wharton well knew, the Mothers are never seen in Goethe's play; they are so powerful and terrifying that we are left only to imagine them. In part 2 of the drama Mephistopheles, pressed by Faust, declares: "Unwilling, I reveal a loftier mystery" than any so far disclosed. "In solitude are throned the Goddesses, No Space around them, Place and Time still less; Only to speak of them embarrasses. They are

THE MOTHERS!" Faust, trembling, insists on descending to
their realm. Mephistopheles says: "Descend, then! I could
also say: Ascend! 'Twere all the same. Escape from the
Created to shapeless forms in liberated spaces!"[3]

Although commentary on the Mothers has always been
bountiful and varied, there has traditionally been little dis-
agreement about their primalness. The Mothers have been
called "the creating and sustaining principle, from which
everything proceeds that has life and form on the surface of
the Earth." They are the "Goddesses, who preside over the
eternal metamorphoses of things, of all that already exists":
the "primitive forms (or ideas) of things—*Urbilder der
Dinge*." They are "the formless realm of the inner world of
spirit—the invisible depth of the mind, struggling to bring
forth its own conceptions"; "the elemental or original material of all forms." The Mothers "are the elements from which
spring all that is corporeal as well as all that is intellectual."[4]

Between Goethe's "Mothers" and Wharton's a century of
scholarship theorized about primordial maternal power, or
matriarchy as it has been called, both mystic and pragmatic.
Most famous of course was Johann Bachofen's *Das Mutterrecht* [The Mother Right], which was published in 1861 and
by the end of the nineteenth century was well known in most
intellectual circles. Joseph Campbell explains how Bachofen's learned teacher, von Savigny, "sent the young Swiss,
Bachofen, off to Rome, to Greece, and beyond, to the realm of
'the mothers' of Goethe's *Faust*."[5] In that imagined realm
Bachofen, a classicist, found the vision that inspired *Das
Mutterrecht*. In his book he asserts that myth and religion
are reliable repositories of truth about the unrecorded past
and argues that preceding the present reign of the patriarchate (that is, the epoch of recorded history), the Western
world was matriarchal. He romanticizes:

The relationship which stands at the origin of all culture, of every
virtue, of every nobler aspect of existence, is that between mother

and child; it operates in a world of violence as the divine principle of love, of union, of peace. Raising her young, the woman learns earlier than the man to extend her loving care beyond the limits of ego to another creature, and to direct whatever gift of invention she possesses to the preservation and improvement of this other's existence. Woman at this stage is the repository of all culture, of all benevolence, of all devotion, of all concern for the living and grief for the dead.[6]

This notion of maternity as the root of culture, best (and first) put by Bachofen but certainly not limited to *Das Mutterrecht* or even to its most direct spin-offs such as Helen Diner's *Mothers and Amazons,* one of many books inspired by Bachofen's in the first three decades of this century, along with Goethe's intimation of female primalness, takes explicit, carnal shape in Wharton's last two novels in the figure of Halo Spear, whose name, true to Wharton's lifelong penchant for symbolic names, yokes beatitude and ferocity.

Vance Weston begins to suspect toward the end of *Hudson River Bracketed* that his grandmother's God-centered perception of life may not be naive: "Perhaps what she called 'God' was the same as what he called 'The Mothers'—that mysterious Sea of Being of which the dark reaches swayed and rumoured in his soul . . . " (p. 449; Wharton's ellipsis). Here Vance begins to mature, but he does not learn the secret of the Mothers until the end of *The Gods Arrive.* On her deathbed, his grandmother imparts her final discovery: " 'Maybe we haven't made enough of pain—been too afraid of it,' she whispered," and Vance realizes that "those last words of his grandmother's might turn out to be the clue of his labyrinth" (pp. 402, 404). They do. After Floss jilts him, Vance renounces women and goes off by himself to a retreat in the woods. There he happens on a copy of Augustine's *Confessions.* When he reads the church father's account of his own attempt to avoid suffering and sacrifice—his effort to evade Christ's call: "I am the Food of the full-grown. Become a man and thou shalt feed on Me"—Vance awakens: "The food of the full-grown—of the full-grown! That was the key to his grandmother's last words. 'Become a man and thou shalt feed on Me' was the message of experience to the soul" (p. 411). This concept of accepting suffering governs his final growth from a confused misogynist boy, afraid of the strong adult (and primal) female, into a potentially mature man and artist. "Yes, it was time to eat of that food; time to grow up; time to fly from his shielded solitude and go down again among" women (p. 412).

The woman who receives him is the expectant mother, Halo. Debilitated by illness and loneliness and self-doubt, the aspiring artist Vance—resuscitated by his grandmother's dying words and Augustine's gloss on them—descends to the life-supporting and therefore art-generating primal Mothers, symbolized by the muselike Halo now pregnant with new life. Vance stammers: " 'I'm not fit for you yet, Halo; I'm only just learning how to walk . . .' " and she "gave a little laugh. 'But then I shall have two children to take care of instead of one!' . . . With a kind of tranquil gravity she lifted up her arms in the ancient attitude of prayer" (p. 432). It is an image older than human history—the image of the mother-goddess in every ancient myth and legend: tranquil and grave, full bodied with the promise of new life, arms raised in strength to the heavens.

All of her life Edith Wharton saw men as weakly affairs. The most common criticism of her fiction has always been that her male characters do not compare with her women, and the charge is just. No man in Wharton's canon can come up to the mark of a Justine Brent or an Ellen Olenska or a Rose Sellars—to name only three out of many. In part the men do not measure up because Wharton's point, exactly, is that patriarchal society has made of men tyrants and fools. But lying even deeper, it must be admitted, has always been her gut-belief in the innate inferiority of men. Not until her last novel, however, in the figure of Halo Tarrant, who partakes of the strength and potency of the Mothers, did Wharton openly confront her own notion of inherent female superiority and develop it into an intellectually provocative, even if fundamentally conservative, concept.

Perhaps it is ironic that it was German literature and scholarship that provided Wharton with her image of the Mothers. During the war, at the same time that she hated the Germans, she reread Goethe and Schiller and pored over older German sagas, almost as if to reassure herself that the German language and literature of which she had been so fond was not of the same mind as the military machine. But whatever her reasons, during the war she turned to Goethe in particular, and his influence lasted through the twenties, showing up first in *The Age of Innocence,* with its opening scene staged against an operatic version of *Faust,* and last in *The Gods Arrive,* with its closing scene evoking—actually invoking for America—the primal Mothers: figures terrifying but also healing in their insistence on confronting rather than avoiding pain and suffering.

Most of her life Edith Wharton imaged pain and anguish as huge black Furies swooping down on her, or on a character, and thus objectified suffering as an enemy, something to be avoided. After the war she changed her mind, and by the time she wrote *Hudson River Bracketed* and *The Gods Arrive* the awful bowel-gripping Furies had turned into the Mothers. Mythically the translation, or transfiguration, makes perfect sense, for the Furies are actually nothing more than patriarchy's negative redefinition of the ancient mother-goddess principle. In the *Oresteia,* which chronicles the installation of patriarchal power, the Furies are the vengeant last agents of the matriarchate, the final defenders of mother-right. They are evil only because they are outlaws: they are the enemies of patriarchy, which is in the process of obliterating maternal power. In the play of the trilogy called *The Furies* Apollo declares that henceforth the father will be the more important parent; the mother will properly be perceived simply as the bearer of the race. The Furies cry out in response "O youthful gods, you have ridden down the ancient laws" and they curse Apollo: "You indeed have overcome the old deities, deceived with wine, the ancient goddesses."[7]

In her last two novels Wharton, it could be said, absorbed rather than feared the Furies. With them, so to speak, she tried to call America back to the ancient Mothers, the awesome matriarchs of Bachofen and then before him Goethe and then before either, so she seems to have believed, all human thought itself.

If this final, highly romantic vision of Wharton's is saddening—and in many ways it is: it conceives of women in totally maternal terms, it writes men off once and for all, it reverses rather than equalizes or eradicates the hierarchy of gender—it is also intriguing. Had Edith Wharton been a younger woman when she came to her theory of the Mothers, might she have moved beyond *Hudson River Bracketed* and *The Gods Arrive* to fiction intellectually and artistically successful in its attempt to posit some sort of spiritual matriarchy? The book she was at work on when she died, *The Buccaneers,* is a lovely fiction about nineteenth-century Americans, one that almost suggests that the aging author was treating herself to a respite from her struggles with postwar problems. It is tempting to imagine that she might have returned to the issues of power, creativity, and healing raised in her last two novels about modern Americans and found a way to harmonize her newly articulated mysticism about femaleness with her old concern for women's lives in the here-and-now. But that perhaps, given the vitality of her argument with America on the subject of women from *The House of Mirth* through *The Age of Innocence,* may be a little like wanting to modernize an old house. Maybe we don't need less than what we have.

Notes

1. Hubert Howe Bancroft, *The Book of the Fair: An Historical and Descriptive Presentation of the World's Science, Art, and Industry as Viewed through the Columbian Exposition at Chicago in 1893*, 2 vols. (New York: Crown Publishers, 1894), 1: 267.

2. *Campbell's Illustrated History of the World's Columbian Exposition in Two Volumes* (Chicago: J. B. Campbell, 1894), 1: 205.

3. Larzer Ziff, *The American 1890's: Life and Times of a Lost Generation* (New York: Viking, 1966), p. 283.

4. R. W. B. Lewis, *Edith Wharton: A Biography* (New York: Harper and Row, 1975), p. 86.

5. Mary Cadwalader Jones wrote chapter 16, "Women's Opportunities in Town and Country" (vol. 2 of *The Woman's Book, Dealing Practically with the Modern Conditions of Home-Life, Self-Support, Education, Opportunities, and Every-Day Problems in Two Volumes* (New York: Charles Scribner's Sons, 1894); in chapter 1 (vol. 1), "Occupations for Women," her article "The Training of a Nurse," which appeared in *Scribner's* magazine for November 1890, is quoted extensively.

6. *The Woman's Book*, 1: 15.

7. Ibid., p. v.

8. Ibid., p. 2.

9. Edith Wharton, *The Collected Short Stories of Edith Wharton*, ed. R. W. B. Lewis, 2 vols. (New York: Charles Scribner's Sons, 1968), 1: 58–59.

10. Edith Wharton, *Bunner Sisters*, in *Xingu and Other Stories* (New York: Charles Scribner's Sons, 1916), pp. 420–21.

11. Edith Wharton, *The Touchstone* (New York: Charles Scribner's Sons, 1900), pp. 18–19.

12. James D. Hart, *The Popular Book: A History of America's Literary Taste* (Berkeley and Los Angeles: University of California Press, 1963), p. 192.

13. Wharton's article on George Eliot appeared in the May 1902 issue of *Bookman*.

14. Cynthia Griffin Wolff, *A Feast of Words: The Triumph of Edith Wharton* (New York: Oxford University Press, 1977), p. 422.

15. Louis Auchincloss, *Edith Wharton* (Minneapolis: University of Minnesota Press, 1961), p. 11.

16. Edith Wharton, *Sanctuary* (New York: Charles Scribner's Sons, 1903), pp., 66–67; Wharton's ellipsis. Further references in the text are to this edition.

1. The body of feminist scholarship at the turn of the century is large and as yet not properly gathered or studied. For my discussion here and elsewhere in this book I've chosen to rely primarily on a representative selection of discursive texts from the period, including: Charlotte Perkins Gilman's *Women and Economics* (1898) and *The Man-Made World, Our Androcentric Culture* (1911), Thorstein Veblen's *The Theory of the Leisure Class* (1899), Hildegarde Hawthorne's *Women and Other Women* (1908), Emily James Putnam's *The Lady: Studies in Certain Significant Phases in Her History* (1910), Anna Garlin Spencer's *Woman's Share in Social Culture* (1912), Mary Roberts Coolidge's *Why Women Are So* (1912), Olive Schreiner's *Woman and Labour* (a best-seller in America in 1912, though Schreiner was South African). This list is only a sampling of feminist argument well known at the time Edith Wharton was writing. For secondary historical commentary, see Aileen S. Kraditor's *The Ideas of the Woman Suffrage Movement 1890-1920* (New York: Columbia University Press, 1965; rpt. Doubleday, 1971) and William L. O'Neill's *Everyone Was Brave: A History of Feminism in America* (New York: Quadrangle, 1969). Both are excellent on the campaign for the vote, but what Kraditor and O'Neill have done for the suffrage literature has not yet been done for the scholarly and theoretical literature of the Woman Movement as a whole between 1890 and 1920 (the sort of books I list above) although it sorely needs doing.

2. Charlotte Perkins Gilman, *Women and Economics: A Study of the Economic Relation between Men·and Women as a Factor in Social Evolution* (Boston: Small, Maynard and Co., 1898; rpt. Harper, 1966), p. 63.

3. Ibid., pp. 14–15.

4. Thorstein Veblen, *The Theory of the Leisure Class: An Economic Study of Institutions* (New York and London: Macmillan, 1899; rpt. Viking, 1965), p. 108.

5. Ibid., p. 101.

6. Eccles. 7: 4.

7. Edith Wharton, *The House of Mirth* (New York: Charles Scribner's Sons, 1905), p. 498. Further references are to this edition.

8. Veblen, *The Theory of the Leisure Class*, p. 60.

9. R. W. B. Lewis, "Introduction," *The House of Mirth* (Boston: Houghton Mifflin, 1963), p. xviii.

10. Emily James Putnam, *The Lady: Studies in Certain Significant Phases in Her History* (New York: G. P. Putnam's Sons, 1910; rpt. University of Chicago Press, 1969), xxxii.

11. Hildegarde Hawthorne, *Women and Other Women: Essays in Wisdom* (New York: Duffield and Co., 1908), p. 218.

12. See, e.g., Hawthorne, *Women and Other Women*, p. 219; Lewis, *Edith Wharton*, p. 181.

13. See Teresa E. Christy, "The Fateful Decade, 1890–1900," *American Journal of Nursing* 75 (July 1975): 1163–66.

14. *The Woman's Book*, 1: 40–41.

15. Ibid., p. 41.

16. Edith Wharton, *The Fruit of the Tree* (New York: Charles Scribner's Sons, 1907), pp. 228–29. Further references are to this edition.

17. *The Fruit of the Tree*, pp. 559, 560. Wharton's use of "lord" here recalls an earlier passage in which Amherst reflects on his conviction that Bessy "would abound in the adaptabilities and pliances which the lords of the earth have seen fit to cultivate in their companions. . . . Amherst had always conveniently supposed that the poet's lines summed up the good woman's rule of ethics: *He for God alone, she for God in him*" (p. 179). The deliberate repetition of "lord" emphasizes how little Amherst's attitude has really changed between his first and second marriages.

18. Blake Nevius, *Edith Wharton: A Study of Her Fiction* (Berkeley and Los Angeles: University of California Press, 1953), p. 104.

19. Hawthorne, *Women and Other Women*, p. 19.

20. Lewis, *Edith Wharton*, p. 155.

21. Millicent Bell, *Edith Wharton and Henry James: The Story of Their Friendship* (New York: George Braziller, 1965), p. 254.

1. Lewis, *Edith Wharton,* p. 207.

2. Ibid., p. 287.

3. Wharton, *The House of Mirth,* p. 194.

4. Edith Wharton, *Ethan Frome* (New York: Charles Scribner's Sons, 1911), p. 27. Page references in the text are to this edition. Worth mentioning here is the fact that some paperback editions of *Ethan Frome,* for example Scribner's 1970 issue, reduce this original ellipsis to a conventional series of thee periods, which is an unfortunate editorial error.

5. As Elizabeth Janeway remarks, "the witch is the shadow and opposite of the loving mother" *(Man's World, Woman's Place: A Study in Social Mythology* [New York: Dell, 1971], p. 126; see also pp. 119, 127–29). Mother is warm, the witch is cold. Mother is soft, the witch is bony. Mother gives, the witch takes away. And so the antitheses run through all the terms of the dichotomy, young/old, beautiful/ugly, fertile/barren, and so forth. Viewed in these terms, both Zeena and the earth itself in *Ethan Frome* serve as mother-antitheses.

6. Michel Carrouges, *"Les Pouvoirs de la femme," Cahiers du Sud* (no. 292), quoted in Simone de Beauvoir, *The Second Sex* (New York: Alfred A. Knopf, 1952; rpt. Bantam, 1961), p. 130.

7. Edith Wharton, Introduction to *Ethan Frome* (New York: Charles Scribner's Sons, 1922), vii.

8. Lionel Trilling, "The Morality of Inertia," *A Gathering of Fugitives* (London: Secker and Warburg, 1957), p. 33.

9. Edwin Bjorkman, *Voices of Tomorrow: Critical Studies of the New Spirit in Literature* (New York and London: Mitchell Kennerley, 1913), pp. 296–97. Bjorkman also sees that romantic love, in addition to economics, is an important theme in the story but, oddly—given how attuned he is to the social criticism of the story, he misses Wharton's point about love; he gathers that she implies marriage to Mattie as the answer to Ethan's problems when, in Bjorkman's opinion, "Romantic love, as idealized for us by our sentimental-minded forefathers, has long ago gone into bankruptcy." He declares: "Had Zeena died and Matt married Ethan—well, it is my private belief that inside of a few years life on that farm would have been practically what it was before Matt arrived, with Matt playing the part of Zeena II—

different, of course, and yet the same" (pp. 301, 303). His "private belief," of course, is not really private at all, but the result of Wharton's construction of her tale.

10. Anna Garlin Spencer, *Woman's Share in Social Culture* (Philadelphia: J. B. Lippincott Co., 1912), pp. 247, 244–46.

11. *The Woman's Book*, 1: 62.

12. Edith Wharton, *A Backward Glance* (New York: D. Appleton-Century, 1934), p. 293.

13. The French version is reprinted in W. D. MacCallan's "The French Draft of *Ethan Frome*," *Yale University Library Gazette* 27 (1952): 40–47. On the date of composition, which R. W. B. Lewis estimates as 1907 and Cynthia Griffin Wolff as either 1906 or 1907, see Lewis, *Edith Wharton*, p. 296; Wolff, *A Feast of Words*, p. 161.

14. "Il [Hart] releva la tête, et vit sa femme qui se dressait, maigre et grelottante, sur le seuil. La lampe à l'huile qu'elle tenait à la main éclairait par en dessous la figure pâle et fatiguée aux traits indécis, mettant des ombres macabres en dessus de ses pommettes, enfonçait les yeux dans leurs orbites, faisait ressortir les creux bleuâtres des tempes dégarnis et donnait au visage insignifiant un aspect menaçant de revenante" (MacCallan, "The French Draft of *Ethan Frome*," p. 41).

15. Bruno Bettelheim, *The Uses of Enchantment: The Meaning and Importance of Fairy Tales* (New York: Alfred A. Knopf, 1976), pp. 199–215.

16. Beauvoir, *The Second Sex*, p. 179.

17. For contrasting interpretation see Cynthia Griffin Wolff's argument that "*The Blithedale Romance* is, ultimately, about Coverdale. Just so, *Ethan Frome*, is about its narrator," an assumption that leads her to observe that *Ethan Frome* "does not tie the disintegration of individual character to larger communal issues" (Wolff, *A Feast of Words*, pp. 164, 370). In fact, Wharton's story (like Hawthorne's) is about large communal issues, and one of the principal ways in which she emphasizes the pervasiveness of the psychosocial problem involved is by giving the story (unlike Hawthorne) to a narrator who is not even a participant in the action, much less the center of interest. He is just an average young man who shares Ethan's fears of woman so deeply that he can serve as a medium to give them expression.

18. "On eût dit qu'elle [Mattie] exprimait toute la sourde angoisse de la longue lignée de femmes qui, depuis deux cents ans,

s'étaient usées la vie et dévorées le coeur dans l'étroite et morne existence de la campagne américaine" (MacCallan, "The French Draft of *Ethan Frome*," p. 47).

19. Charlotte Perkins Gilman, *The Man-Made World, or Our Androcentric Culture* (New York: Charlton Co., 1911), pp. 96, 97, 98, 102.

20. Edith Wharton, *The Reef* (New York: D. Appleton and Co., 1912), p. 86. Further references are to this edition.

21. MS. of "The Reef," copyright 1912, renewed 1940 William R. Tyler (Edith Wharton Papers in the Collection of American Literature, the Beinecke Rare Book and Manuscript Library, Yale University), pp. 135, back; 50, back; 1 ff.

22. Putnam, *The Lady*, p. xxxii.

23. Louis Auchincloss, Introduction to *The Reef* (New York: Charles Scribner's Sons, 1965), p. v.

24. Hawthorne, *Women and Other Women*, pp. 26, 27.

25. Simone de Beauvoir's comment on mythic animism is interesting here: "Man finds . . . in woman bright stars and dreamy moon, the light of the sun, the shade of grottoes; and, conversely, the wild flowers of thickets, the proud garden rose are women. Nymphs, dryads, sirens, undines, fairies haunt the fields and woods, the lakes, oceans, moorland. Nothing lies deeper in the hearts of men than this animism. . . . It is sometimes asserted that these comparisons reveal sexual sublimation; but rather they express an affinity between woman and the elements that is as basic as sexuality itself. Man expects something other than the assuagement of instinctive cravings from the possession of a woman: she is the privileged object through which he subdues Nature" (*The Second Sex*, p. 145).

26. Ibid., pp. 171–72.

27. Ibid., p. 132.

1. Putnam, *The Lady*, p. 69.

2. Gilman, *Women and Economics*, p. 71.

3. Edmund Wilson, *The Wound and the Bow: Seven Studies in Literature* (Boston: Houghton Mifflin, 1929), pp. 202.

4. Edith Wharton, *The Custom of the Country* (New York: Scribner's, 1913), p. 89. Further references are to this edition.

5. See, Bell, *Edith Wharton and Henry James*, p. 242.

6. Hawthorne, *Women and Other Women*, p. 35.

7. Bancroft, *The Book of the Fair*, 1: 267, 269.

8. Olive Schreiner, *Woman and Labour* (London: T. Fisher Unwin, 1911), pp. 144–45, 147.

9. Frances Hodgson Burnett, *The Shuttle*, (New York: Frederick A. Stokes, 1906), pp. 74–75.

10. Ibid., p. 294.

11. Veblen, *The Theory of the Leisure Class*, p. 63.

12. As Eva Figes puts it for a modern audience (repeating of course the argument made by Gilman and others), "it is important to remember that, although we may regard marriage with dependence as a form of slavery, for the woman of the past it was regarded as the only possible form of freedom—it was only through marriage that she could become a woman in her own right in the eyes of the world, and much depended on finding a tolerable and reasonably tolerant mate" (*Patriarchal Attitudes* [Greenwich, Conn.: Fawcett, 1970], p. 74).

13. Gilman, *The Man-Made World*, p. 38.

14. Spencer, *Woman's Share in Social Culture*, p. 28.

15. See William Wasserstrom, *Heiress of All the Ages: Sex and Sentiment in the Genteel Tradition* (Minneapolis: University of Minnesota Press, 1959), p. 56.

16. For the distinction between these two methods of displaying upperclass status, conspicuous leisure or conspicuous consumption, see Veblen, *The Theory of the Leisure Class*, pp. 85–86.

17. Lewis, *Edith Wharton*, p. 349.

18. Edith Wharton, *A Backward Glance* (New York: D. Appleton-Century, 1934), p. 176.

19. The divorce issue during the Progressive Era, an issue that inevitably reflected conflicting attitudes toward the institutions of marriage and the family and often split down feminist and antifeminist lines, is the subject of an excellent study by William L. O'Neill, *Divorce in the Progressive Era* (New Haven: Yale University Press, 1967).

1. Orison Swett Marden, *Woman and Home* (New York: Thomas Y. Crowell, 1915), pp. 3–4.

2. Ibid., pp. 13, 15–16.

3. Edith Wharton, *The House of Mirth* (New York: Charles Scribner's Sons, 1905), p. 17.

4. Lewis, *Edith Wharton*, p. 371.

5. Ibid., p. 388.

6. Edith Wharton, *Fighting France, from Dunkerque to Belfort* (New York: Charles Scribner's Sons, 1915), p. 33.

7. Edith Wharton, *Summer* (New York: D. Appleton, 1917), pp. 9, 12. References in the text are to this edition.

8. Phyllis Chesler, *Women and Madness* (New York: Avon, 1973), pp. 20, 30.

9. The "Beatrice Palmato" fragment is reprinted in Wolff, *A Feast of Words*, pp. 301–5, and in Lewis's biography of Wharton, pp. 545–48.

10. Wolff, *A Feast of Words*, pp. 306–7.

11. For the contrasting arguments see Wolff, pp. 407–15, and Lewis, p. 544.

12. Edith Wharton, *In Morocco* (New York: Charles Scribner's Sons, 1920), pp. 178, 193, 192, 195.

13. Edith Wharton, *The Age of Innocence* (New York: D. Appleton and Co., 1920), pp. 292–93. References in the text are to this edition.

14. Putnam, *The Lady*, p. 3, emphasis mine.

15. Edith Wharton, *A Backward Glance* (New York: D. Appleton-Century, 1934), p. 22.

16. Edith Wharton, *French Ways and Their Meaning* (New York: D. Appleton, 1919), pp. 100–102.

17. Edith Wharton, *Old New York* (New York: Charles Scribner's Sons, 1924), p. 251.

18. Gilman, *The Man-Made World*, pp. 163–64.

19. Louis Auchincloss, *Edith Wharton: A Woman in Her Time* (New York: Viking, 1971), p. 128.

20. Sir James George Frazer, *The Golden Bough: A Study in Magic and Religion* (New York: Macmillan, 1922), p. 154. The "state of society" Frazer imagines is properly labeled matriarchal rather than simply matrilineal because of his statement that it is a system where "descent through the mother is *everything*" (emphasis mine); in a merely matrilineal system, descent through the mother counts for a great deal but finally falls short of counting for "everything" (as descent through the father in a patriarchy does, for example).

21. Lewis, *Edith Wharton*, p. 433.

22. Wharton, *A Backward Glance*, pp. 147–48.

23. Ibid., p. 148.

24. David Graham Phillips, *Susan Lenox, Her Fall and Rise* (New York: D. Appleton and Co., 1917; rpt. Popular Library, 1978), pp. 591, 649.

25. Lewis, *Edith Wharton*, pp. 504–5.

1. Lewis, *Edith Wharton*, p. 396.

2. Edith Wharton, *The Glimpses of the Moon* (New York: D. Appleton and Co., 1922), pp. 345, 319. References in the text are to this edition.

3. Edith Wharton, *The Mother's Recompense* (New York: D. Appleton and Co., 1925), p. 73. References in the text are to this edition.

4. Edith Wharton, *Twilight Sleep* (New York: D. Appleton and Co., 1927), pp. 297, 134. References in the text are to this edition.

5. See Nevius, *Edith Wharton*, pp. 219–20, 258.

6. Quoted in Lewis, *Edith Wharton*, p. 527.

7. Quoted in Percy Lubbock, *Portrait of Edith Wharton* (New York and London: D. Appleton-Century, 1947), p. 148.

8. Edith Wharton, *A Son at the Front* (New York: Charles Scribner's Sons, 1923), p. 154; Wharton's ellipsis.

9. Lewis, *Edith Wharton*, p. 369.

10. Margaret Deland, *Small Things* (New York: D. Appleton and Co., 1919), p. 98.

11. Jane Addams, *The Long Road of Woman's Memory* (New York: Macmillan, 1916), xiv.

12. Lewis, *Edith Wharton*, p. 424.

13. Edith Wharton, *The Children* (New York: D. Appleton and Co., 1928), p. 105. References in the text are to this edition.

14. Especially pertinent to the discussion here is Elizabeth Janeway's analysis of the psychological complexity of the human infantile experience and the myths to which it gives rise in *Man's World, Woman's Place: A Study in Social Mythology* (New York: Dell, 1971), chapters 3–5.

15. Leslie Fiedler, *Love and Death in the American Novel* (New York: Dell, 1960), p. 339.

16. Katharine M. Rogers, *The Troublesome Helpmate: A History*

of Misogyny in Literature (Seattle and London: University of Washington Press, 1966), p. 37.

17. MS. of "The Children" in the Edith Wharton Collection at the Beinecke Library, Yale University, p. 80, back.

18. Wharton, *Twilight Sleep*, pp. 32, 35, 255–56; Wharton's ellipses except for the second.

19. Ibid., p. 13.

1. Lewis, *Edith Wharton*, p. 512.

2. Edith Wharton, *Hudson River Bracketed* (New York: D. Appleton and Co., 1929), p. 336. The concept of the Mothers recurs throughout Wharton's last two novels. For other references see *Hudson River Bracketed*, p. 391; and *The Gods Arrive* (New York: D. Appleton and Co., 1932), pp. 23, 72, 118, 380. Citations in the text are to these editions of the two novels.

3. Johann Wolfgang von Goethe, *Faust, the Second Part,* trans. Bayard Taylor (Boston: James R. Osgood and Co., 1871), pp. 89, 93.

4. These interpretations are a composite of standard nineteenth-century views, such as those that might have influenced Wharton herself as a young woman. They are taken from Bayard Taylor's notes to the edition of *Faust* cited above, pp. 459–63.

5. Joseph Campbell, Introduction to *Myth, Religion, and Mother Right* (Princeton, N.J.: Princeton University Press, 1967), p. xxxvii.

6. Johann Bachofen, *Mother Right,* in *Myth, Religion, and Mother Right,* trans. Ralph Manheim, p. 79.

7. Aeschylus, *The Furies,* in *The Tragedies of Aeschylus,* trans. Theodore Alois Buckley (London: Henry G. Bohn, 1849), p. 201.

Index